Guitar Chord Guru

The Chord Book
Your Guide For Success!

By Karl Aranjo

Catalog #07-4078

ISBN 978-1-56922-159-4

Cover Art Direction by Matt Haag
Cover photo by James Bean, Ojai, CA
Cover photo of Jay McArthur

CREATIVE CONCEPTS
PUBLISHING

EXCLUSIVELY DISTRIBUTED BY

HAL•LEONARD®
CORPORATION
7777 W. BLUEMOUND RD. P.O. BOX 13819 MILWAUKEE, WI 53213

Visit Hal Leonard Online at
www.halleonard.com

Welcome

You're holding one in a series of exciting new **reference** books from Creative Concepts publishing: *Guitar Chord Guru.* Each book bearing this name is incredibly clear, informative and practical. This material has been carefully tested on hundreds of students and yields fantastic results while appearing to be fun and easy. For today's students and teachers, this series of educational materials represents the best available!!

Special note to teachers . . .

If you're a professional guitar teacher, you've no doubt been frustrated with traditional guitar books. Most students don't like them and simply won't study them. Aware that the tired old methods of the past don't measure up, students who have these books forced upon them usually quit their guitar lessons.

The newer books are a little better but often contain only a few worthwhile pages and generally don't fit in with your program. You've always felt stifled by them because they won't allow you to teach *your way.*

These excellent *reference books* solve these problems beautifully because they allow you to focus your lessons on the material essential to developing real world playing skills without breaking your rhythm. The *easygrid©* graphics were created especially for this project and are unavailable elsewhere. The diagrams and illustrations in this book are like a breath of fresh air, making teaching and learning a pleasure again.

Special note to students . . .

If you're serious about learning today's guitar, then you need to have current, top notch material created with someone like you in mind. The book you're holding is *the* serious choice - not just another waste of time and money. Every page of **Karl Aranjo's** book contains only the essential material you want and deserve with none of the bull.

Because this a *reference book* and **is** **not** part of a "graded" method book series (Book 1, Book 2, etc.) you learn only what **you** want to learn when **you** want to learn it. Each book is an intensive study providing a wealth of material in specific key areas. This series keeps you motivated and enables you to concentrate your efforts where you see fit, keeping **you** in total control of your developing style.

Table of Contents

Basic Open String Chords

E Ma, Emi & E7 1
A Ma, Ami & A7 1
G Ma, & G7 2
C Ma, & C7 2
B7, B9, & B7 #9 2
D Ma, Dmi & D7 3
F Ma, & Fmi 3
How to practice chords 4
Cadences 5
Applicable song list 6
Chord quality, Chord symbols 7
Advanced open string chords, Chord reference charts 8
How to substitute chords 17

Barre Chords

Essential guitar theory 18
Root 5 & Root 6 thinking 22
Barre chord development 24
Theory of movable chords 25
Origin and fingerings of Root 6 & Root 5 barre chords 28
Mastering and moving Root 6 & Root 5 barre chords 32
Alternate voicings 40
Critical concepts 41

Music Theory, Chord Theory

The Major scale, half & whole steps 45
Flat keys & Sharp keys 48
Circle of fifths 50

Jazz Chords, Advanced Chords

Advanced Major chord alterations 54
Advanced minor chord alterations 56
Advanced Dominant 7 chord alterations 58
minor line clichés 60
Major line clichés 63

Gaining theoretical expertise

Understanding the musical staff 66
Complete notes of the guitar in tab & standard notation 68
Key signatures 70
Theoretical basis of chords 72
Theory of Diminished & Augmented chords 74
Diatonic & compound intervals 77
Chord formulas & spellings 79
Slash chords - (G/B, C/D, D/F# etc....) 82
Suspended 7 & 11th chords 84

Five position thinking

C Major super pattern & 5 positions of C Major 86
G Major super pattern & 5 positions of G Major 88
5 positions of A, B, D, E & F Major 92
Converting the 5 basic shapes to minor 95
Converting the 5 basic shapes to dominant 7 chords 98
Practicing the 5 basic shapes 101

Synonomous chords & common knowledge substitutions

Synonymous chord formations 102
Sus 2 & add 9 chords 103
Diminished 7 & Dominant 7 (b9) chords 104

The World of Music Revolves Around Chords and Chord Progressions

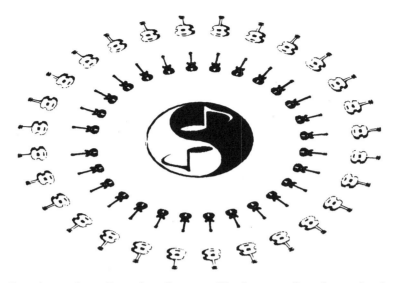

Guitar playing is physical . . . Guitar playing is intellectual

This means that a guitarist needs to master a lot of specific **chord** fingerings and shapes. At the same time, one must develop an understanding of the theory behind these chords in order to have fun with them and develop one's own sound. Since all music, including pop, rock, jazz, blues, metal, classical and alternative is ultimately based on chords, an excellent and thorough working knowledge of them is essential. Study this book until you know how to play and GIVE NAMES to a fair amount of new and exciting chords. When you feel as though you've reached a plateau in your learning and playing, return to the **Guitar Chord Guru.**

This **reference book** is *truly one of a kind* because it shows you the nuts and bolts of guitar playing while allowing you as a student or teacher, to do things your own way. Beginning, advanced and career guitarists will find this little book to be one of the most valuable tools in their entire arsenal. Both challenging and enjoyable, this is the *book you've been looking for.*

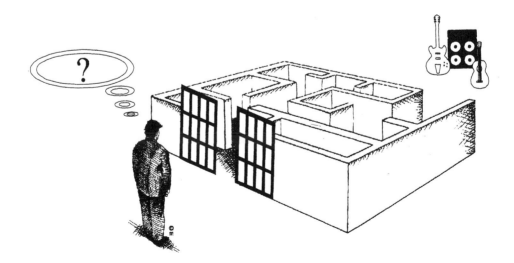

KARL W. ARANJO is a professional guitarist and guitar instructor based in Southern California. His lifelong guitar studies have included teachers such as Tony Mottolla, Ted Greene & the late William G. Leavitt, author of the Berklee method.

Karl is a graduate of Boston's Berklee College of Music and the leader of a busy performing band, ***Karl Aranjo's Jazz Attack.*** When not teaching, learning, performing, writing or recording, Karl enjoys the company of his lovely wife Karen and their small unruly terrier, Roxanne.

Mr. Aranjo welcomes any and all correspondence which may be directed to Creative Concepts Publishing.

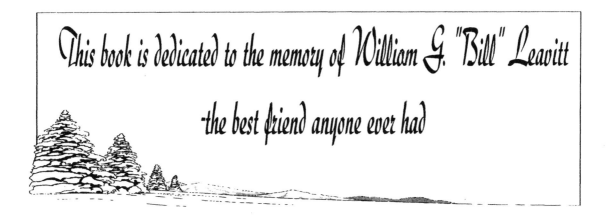

This book is dedicated to the memory of William G. "Bill" Leavitt
-the best friend anyone ever had

(SPECIAL THANKS TO MY STUDENT GRAHAM RUBY, FOR THE TERRIFFIC JOB OF PROOFREADING.)

Key- Nomenclature

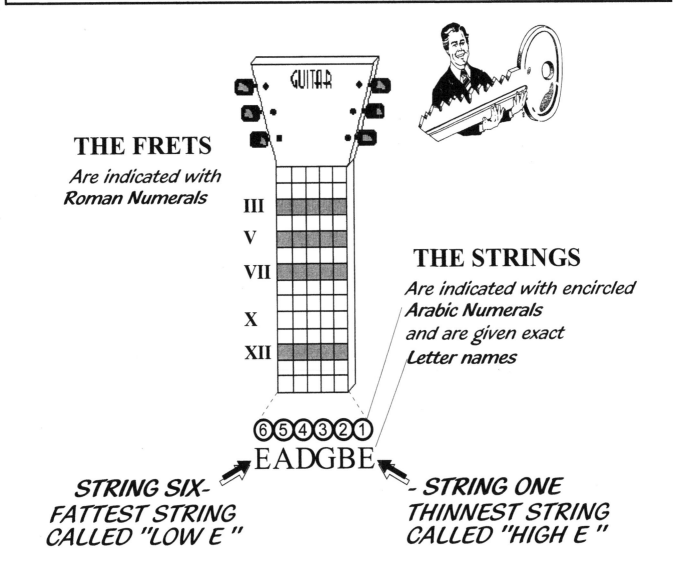

THE FRETS

Are indicated with Roman Numerals

III
V
VII
X
XII

THE STRINGS

Are indicated with encircled Arabic Numerals and are given exact Letter names

⑥⑤④③②①
EADGBE

STRING SIX- FATTEST STRING CALLED "LOW E"

- STRING ONE THINNEST STRING CALLED "HIGH E"

THE FINGERS

Of the **left hand** (fretting hand) are labeled with regular arabic numerals:
1, 2, 3, 4, & th (for the thumb)

Of the **right hand** (picking hand) are labeled with letters:
P, I, M, A, E.

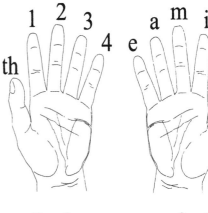

left   *right*

Key- How to read the chord graphs

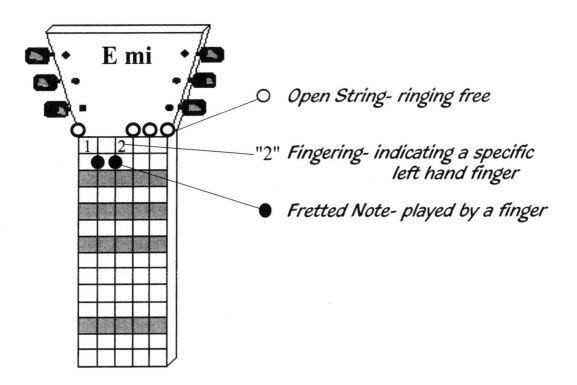

E mi

○   *Open String- ringing free*

"2"   *Fingering- indicating a specific left hand finger*

●   *Fretted Note- played by a finger*

Typical chord diagrams like the ones found in all guitar books and magazines.

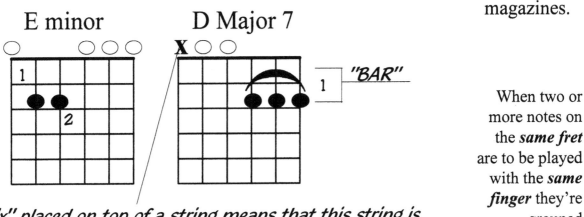

E minor   **D Major 7**

"BAR"

When two or more notes on the *same fret* are to be played with the *same finger* they're grouped together using a thick curved line.

"x" placed on top of a string means that this string is NOT to be played with this particular chord- skip it.

In Summary...

THE FINGERS- Are diagrammed with regular Arabic numerals.

THE FRETS- Are diagrammed with Roman numerals.

THE STRINGS- Are diagrammed with encircled Arabic numerals.

THE CHORD BOOK

This book is all about chords, **how to play them** & **what to call them**. Included is a detailed examination of all the essential theory involved with playing and writing contemporary guitar music in the most musical and logical way possible.

Using this **reference book** is the answer to a prayer for players and teachers. It's simple:

> *Keep teaching the way you're teaching & keep playing the way you're playing.*

When you're interested in some particular chord or theoretical concept, look it up in the extensive table of contents. This allows you to return to your business without getting hooked into some structured series of method books that don't fit in with your style...books that are of **LITTLE OR NO INTEREST** to *you* , the player.

Those who are self-taught traditionally concentrate their efforts on **learning to play songs**. This means faithfully reproducing guitar parts found on recordings and rhythmically strumming the *chord changes* in songbooks. Thus, the most important skills for the guitarist involve quite a bit of specialized knowledge in the areas of chords and musical theory. This is exactly the information revealed in the pages of the reference manual you're holding.

If you **are** a teacher the material presented here can be your secret weapon. Each page quickly imparts critical concepts and allows you to continue teaching without drawing a ton of circles, arrows, written words and chord graphs. *At last,* all the essential diagrams, drawings and information concerning theory, chords and their uses in one logical, easy to read book. The printed material in these pages is simply the **best**! Here it is...

"The book you've been looking for."

Also Now Available

From Karl Aranjo - *"Your Guru for the Guitar"*

Guitar Scale Guru

The Scale Book
Your Guide For Success!

Catalog #07-4088

VIII

ISBN# 1-56922-186-3

Basic Open String Chords: E & A

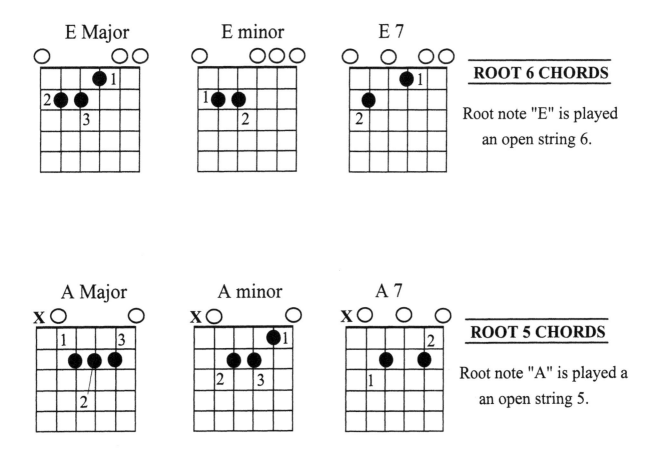

E Major **E minor** **E 7**

ROOT 6 CHORDS

Root note "E" is played
an open string 6.

A Major **A minor** **A 7**

ROOT 5 CHORDS

Root note "A" is played a
an open string 5.

Important Notes:

The ***Root note*** of a chord is the note which gives a particular chord its name. For example, the root note of an **E major**, **E minor** or **E 7** chord is the single note "E". The root note of a chord is usually the note with the lowest pitch and can also be thought of as the ***"bass note"***.

Chords are often categorized according to the string on which their root note is located. The **A Major, A minor** and **A7** chords diagrammed above are said to be ***Root 5 chords*** because their root note, the single note "A", is an open fifth string.

The **E Major, E minor** and **E7** chords diagrammed above are said to be ***Root 6 chords*** because their root note, the single note "E", is an open sixth string.

Basic Open Chords: G &C

G Major
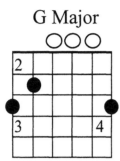

G 7
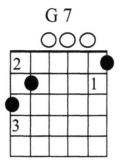

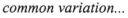
ROOT 6 CHORDS

Root note "G" is played
on string 6, fret III .

common variation...
G Major
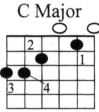

C Major
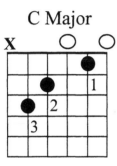

C 7
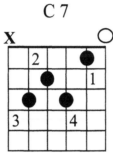

ROOT 5 CHORDS

Root note "C" is played
on string 5, fret III .

common variation...
C Major
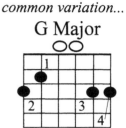

First Position Chords: B

B 7
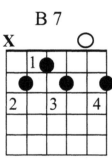

B 9
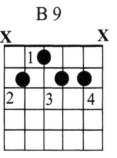

B 7 #9

ROOT 5 CHORDS

Root note "B" is played
on string 5, fret II .

Notes:

Chords of the ***Dominant 7*** classification (such as the **B7, B9 & B7#9** pictured above) are some of the most useful and powerful chords in music, learn them well.

The type of chord sound most often associated with the music of **Jimi Hendrix** is the **dominant 7 # 9**. ***B7 #9*** is an example of this chord sound.

D Major
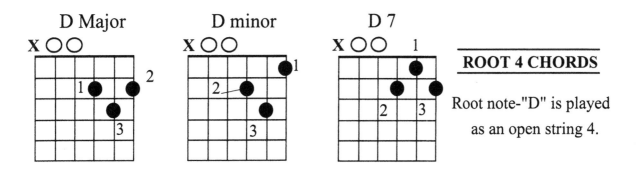

X O O

D minor

X O O

D 7

X O O   1

ROOT 4 CHORDS

Root note-"D" is played

as an open string 4.

First Position Chords: F

F Major *

X X   1

F minor *

X X   1

ROOT 4 CHORDS

Root note-"F" is located

on string 4, fret III.

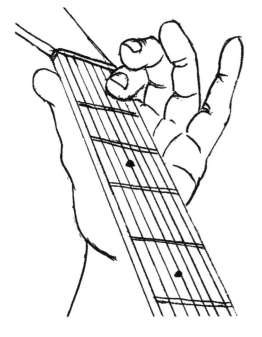

Note:

Any chord can easily be mastered by changing the position of your wrist and/ or elbow while playing. The position and *feel* of your entire arm changes with each new chord. Learn to control the fine movements of your **wrist and elbow**, paying close attention to the *feeling* of each chord or series of chords. Guitar playing is a physical activity which involves far more than just the fingers.

F Major for example is a very difficult chord to learn because of the partial barre on fret I. Most people increase the leverage of their first finger by moving their elbow towards the body.

How to practice chords

Chord formations are often referred to as *"shapes"* or *"grips"*. These terms are very telling and quite useful. As I have illustrated, each chord has a shape or little picture associated with it. These pictures are totally unique but often bear similarities to one another. For example, **A Major, A 7** and **A minor** are very alike in appearance and even have some notes in common. One way to develop a good chord vocabulary is to study and learn new chords in relation to the ones you already know, taking little mental snapshots along the way.

The word "grip" makes me think of the actual physical nature of a chord and the feeling it causes in my ***wrist and elbow***. The 18 chords presented thus far in this book are the most basic material imaginable for any guitarist. Practice these chords in super slow motion until you know them as well as you know your phone number. Knowing these chords means you can smoothly and **effortlessly** switch from one to another in the blink of an eye. Knowing these chords means that you can slowly strum your guitar, hearing all the proper open strings and fretted notes clearly ringing out without any buzz, rattle or dead notes.

Changing from chord to chord in an smooth, efficient manner is the name of the game. Practice any series of chord transitions in a deliberate, analytical and thoughtful way. Let's say you wanted to play a song that switched from an A mi chord to a G Major chord over and over.

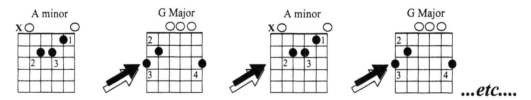

...etc....

When I play this ***chord progression*** I usually:

    ♪ Grip the A mi paying attention to the two open strings.

    ♪ Change to G Major by first picking up finger 1...

    ♪ Continue by moving finger 2 over to the next thickest string...

    ♪ Pick up the 3rd finger, arching and stretching until it comes to rest on the third fret of the thickest string...

    ♪ Bend my 4th finger (pinkie) down towards the ground and bring the center of the fingertip to firmly rest on string one, fret III...

    ♪ As I rearrange my 4th finger I also move my elbow and wrist, bending them both away from my body...

This is an in depth study of seven separate motions, ***and therefore thoughts***, that are needed to make a seamless, flowing transition from **A minor** to **G Major.** For learning to occur, each movement that you're trying to commit to memory must be reduced to a thought during your practice sessions- not just carelessly run over. Changing from **A minor** to **G Major** is not just one thing- it's at least *seven things!*

Practice your chords is super slow motion, making a mental note of every single thing you do, no matter how insignificant it may seem. This is one of the secrets of learning to play an instrument

Cadences

A *cadence* is the sound of musical resolution we hear at the end of a series of two or more chords. When a chord progression makes sense to your ear, that progression has *cadenced*. All songs in all musical styles are made up of cadences. Cadences make the world of music go around.

There are certain cadences that are very standard, ideas that are used countless times in popular songs. Below are some standard chord sequences playable with the basic chords. Strum them with a strong sense of rhythm, you'll need them forever:

Count & Beat your foot:

|1	2	3	4		1, 2, 3, 4	|1	2	3	4		1, 2, 3, 4	
	E		B7			E		E		A			E	
	A		E7			A		A		D			A	
	D		A7			D		D		G			D	
	G		D7			G		G		C			C	
	C		G7			C		C		F			C	
	F		C7			F								

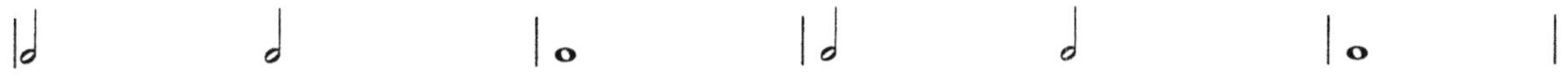

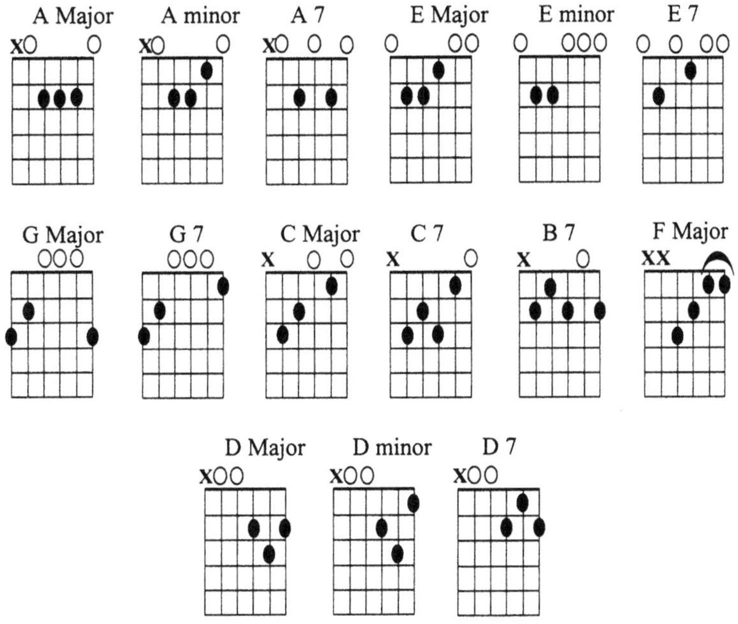

A Major   A minor   A 7   E Major   E minor   E 7

G Major   G 7   C Major   C 7   B 7   F Major

D Major   D minor   D 7

These same cadences are being constantly recycled into one hit tune after another. There are thousands of great songs that use only the chord sequences on this page.

All guitarists must have a good working knowledge of cadences. Mastering the exercises illustrated here will get you off to an excellent start!

Songs playable with the basic open string chords

Bryan Adams
Everything I do...For You

Allman Brothers
One Way Out
Please Be With Me

Bangles
Walk Like An Egyptian

Bad company
Feel Like Making Love
Shooting Star

Beatles
Act Naturally
Get Back
Here Comes The Sun
Let It Be
She Loves You
She Said.
Yellow Submarine
Give Peace A Chance
Maxwells Silver Hammer
Polythene Pam
..many more

Jackson Browne
Take It Easy

Black Sabbath
Paranoid

Blind Melon
Change
No rain

Chuck Berry
Almost Grown
My Ding A Ling

Blondie
Heart of glass
The tide is high

David Bowie
Heroes
Ziggy Stardust

Jimmy Buffett
Biloxi
Ballad Of Spider John
Margaritaville
Great Filling Station

Johnny cash
Big river

Eric Clapton
Before You Accuse Me
Farther On Up The Road
Lay Down Sally

Wonderful Tonight

Clash
Bankrobber
I Fought The Law

Cranberries
Linger

Mary Chapin-Carpenter
Down At The Twist And Shout
Downtown Train
Middle Ground
He Thinks He'll Keep Her
Shut Up And Kiss Me

C.C.R.
Bad Moon Rising
Ever Seen Rain?
Out My Back Door
..many more

Johnny Cash
Boy Named Sue
..many more

Neil Diamond
Solitary Man

Bob Dylan
The Mighty Quinn
All Along Watchtower
Knockin Heavens Door
Like A Rolling Stone
Mr. Tambourine Man
The Times They Are A Changing
...many more

Doors
People Are Strange

John Denver
Leaving On A Jetplane
..many more

Peter Gabriel
Secret World
Solsbury Hill
Washing Of The Water

Grateful Dead
Friend Of The Devil
Uncle Johns Band

Guns N' Roses
Patience

Indigo girls
Reunion
Daddys All Gone

Everybodys Waiting
Power Of Two
Blood And Fire

INXS
Back On Line
Suicide Blonde
Mystify

Billy Joel
River Of Dreams

Arlo Guthrie
Motorcycle Song
..many more

Woody Guthrie
This Land Is Your Land
..many more

Pearl Jam
Elderly Woman

REM
You Are The Everything

Carol King
Up On The Roof

Gordon Lightfoot
Ballad Yarmouth Castle
For Lovin Me

Lyle Lovett
Baltimore
Simple Song

Don Mclean
American Pie
Vincent

Rolling Stones
As Tears Go By
Honky Tonk Women
You Can't Always Get What you Want

Neil Young
Country home
Over And Over
Unknown Legend

Los Lobos
One Time One Night
La Bamba

Nils Lofgren
Moontears

Lynyrd Skynyrd
Ballad Of Curtis Loew
Tuesdays Gone
Simple Man

Sweet Home Alabama

Barry Mcguire
Eve Of Destruction

John Mellencamp
Jack And Diane
R.O.C.K. In The U.S.A.

Bob Seger
Old Time Rock & Roll
...many more

Bruce Springsteen
Cadillac Ranch
Glory Days
Highway Patrol
Human Touch
Independance Day
Living Proof.
My Home Town

Cat Stevens
But I Might Die Tonight
...many more

Paul Simon
Me And Julio
...many more

Traveling Wilburys
End Of The Line

Neil Young
Harvest Moon
Helpless
Mr. Soul

ALSO:
At The Hop
Bang A Gong
Come Go With Me
Don't Be Cruel
Don't You (frgt abt me)
Hey Joe
Jane Says
King Of The Road
Louie Louie
Monster Mash
Not Fade Away
Rock On
Sea Of Love
Stand By Me
Steppin Stone
Spirit In The Sky
Summertime Blues
Surfin U.S.A.
Teenager In Love
That'll Be The Day
Turn! Turn! Turn!
Under The Boardwalk
The Wanderer
Whiter Shade Of Pale
Who Do You Love?
Wild Thing

..many, many more well known songs by just about any group use only the basic chords & cadences

Chord Quality

The *Quality* of a chord is the general overall sound that it makes. The chord reference charts in this book *(beginning on page 9)* have the individual, basic chord types grouped into larger *families* of chords. All of the chords in a **family** produce the same type of sound and are said to possess the same **quality**.

In music, there are three basic types *(families)* of chord sounds:

MAJOR, MINOR & DOMINANT 7.

MAJOR CHORDS are bright, strong and somewhat powerful. The Major chord is the most common chord sound in rock and pop music. Think of the first three notes of the *Star Spangled Banner* or great old rock songs like *Proud Mary* and *All Right Now*. The full, ringing sound of a Major chord just seems right somehow.

MINOR CHORDS sound dark, sad, gloomy, mournful or mysterious. The minor chord sound is heard in the infamous intro of *Stairway to Heaven* and as the first chord in *House of the Rising Sun.*

DOMINANT SEVEN CHORDS are the funky, bluesy types of chord sounds that we associate with the music of B.B. King, Muddy Waters, and all the great bluesman. The Dominant seven chord is **not strictly a blues chord**, however. The purpose of a dominant seven chord is to produce movement in any and all types of music. Without dominant sevenenth chord sounds, the world would be a very strange place.

Common Symbols

Musicians and composers have several different symbols that mean the same thing. All of the symbols in each individual column are interchangeable.

MAJOR CHORDS	MINOR CHORDS	DOMINANT CHORDS
C	C-	C7
C Ma	C m	C dom. 7
C △	C mi	

Advanced Chord Voicings

There are scores of beautiful sounding chords in each of the three basic families of chord quality *(Major, minor & Dominant)*. These chords, called **extended harmonies,** can make guitar playing wondrous and exciting. The basic chords, although tremendously useful and enjoyable, are no way to go through life. All proficient, accomplished guitarists have a computer mind when it comes to chords and are constantly updating their files. <u>**You can never know enough chords**</u>.

Each individual chord has a number of different versions called **voicings**. The song *Moondance* by Van Morrison for example, starts and ends with an **A minor 7** chord. Any one of the following voicings will be useful depending on the effect you want to create and the sounds being made by other musicians who are playing with you.

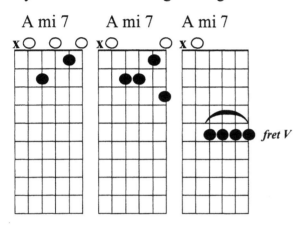

Each one of these three voicings of A mi 7 at left will accomplish the cool, jazzy **A minor 7** chord sound in its own sweet way. This sound has made the song a favorite for over 20 years!

Any chord in the A mi family may be useful in certain circumstances. For an ending try the sweet harp-like sound of this chord:

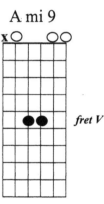

An in depth knowledge of chord voicings is essential to the beautiful art of music making.

Chord Reference Charts

On the pages that follow are numerous advanced and unusual chord voicings that use open strings and are playable within the first 5 frets. Study them slowly as you advance through the rest of the book. Sometimes just one new chord can be the inspiration for an original song or unique arrangement of an old favorite.

Memorizing the names, uses and shapes of the chords is your current focus. **Why** and **how** the chords are named will only distract you from this purpose. All the action is on the neck of your guitar. If you have questions like: "Why is called A mi 9?" and "What makes a chord Major or minor?" refer to the sections on music theory beginning on pages 45 & 66.

Use the reference charts the way you would use a dictionary or encyclopedia.

A painter has a color palette which he uses to create subtle shades and moods. A master chef has his secret recipes and exotic spices. A guitarist uses a wide range of intriguing & exciting sounds to do, that voodoo, that they do so well.

Advanced first position chords

E Major Family

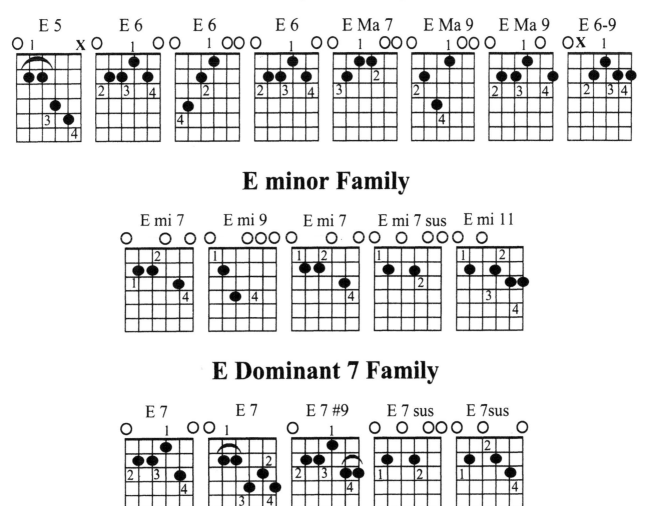

E minor Family

E Dominant 7 Family

E Suspended Chords & E 11th Chords

A special category of chords with a beautiful, glassy sound called **suspended chords** exists. Not generally thought of as Major chords, *"sus. chords"* quite often function as dominant chords but can also be used to create a minor chord sound. For **suspended chords** and **11th** chords keep the following guidelines in mind:

> **E 7 sus** *is the same as* **E mi 7 sus.....**
> **E 11 is *NOT* the same as** **E mi 11**

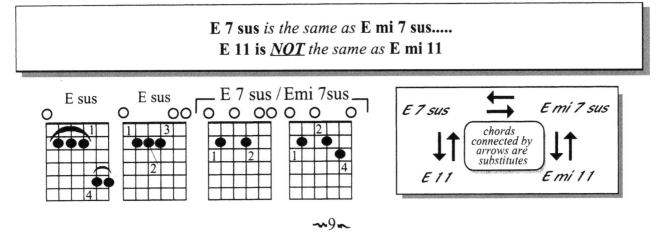

~9~

See page 84 for a complete discussion of suspended 7th & 11th chords.

Advanced first position chords

A Major Family

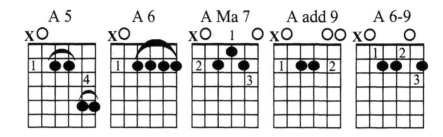

A 5   A 6   A Ma 7   A add 9   A 6-9

A minor Family

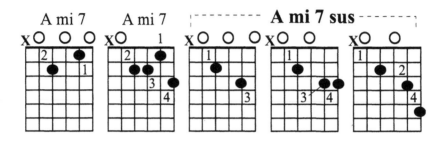

A mi 7   A mi 7   - - - - - - - **A mi 7 sus** - - - - - - -

A Dominant 7 Family

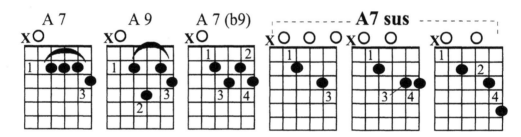

A 7   A 9   A 7 (b9)   - - - - - - - **A7 sus** - - - - - - -

A Suspended Chords

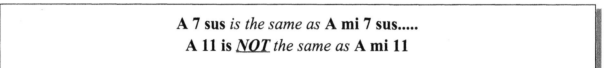

A 7 sus *is the same as* **A mi 7 sus**.....
A 11 is _NOT_ *the same as* **A mi 11**

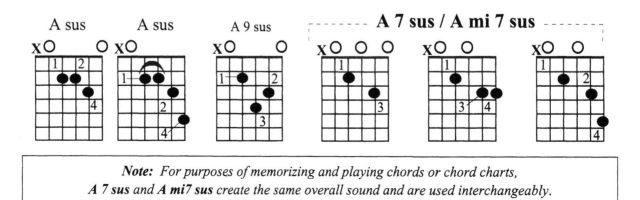

A sus   A sus   A 9 sus   - - - - - **A 7 sus / A mi 7 sus** - - - - -

Note: *For purposes of memorizing and playing chords or chord charts,*
A 7 sus and A mi7 sus create the same overall sound and are used interchangeably.

Advanced first position chords

D Major Family

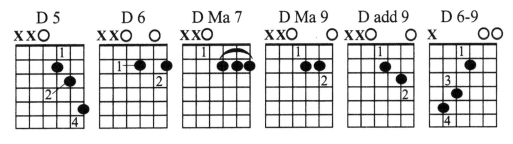

D 5   D 6   D Ma 7   D Ma 9   D add 9   D 6-9

D minor Family

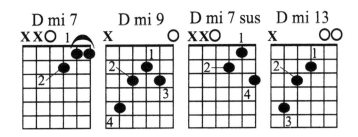

D mi 7   D mi 9   D mi 7 sus   D mi 13

D Dominant 7 Family

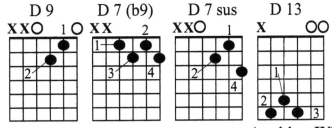

D 9   D 7 (b9)   D 7 sus   D 13

(position IV)

D Suspended Chords

D 7 sus *is the same as* **D mi 7 sus**.....
D 11 is *NOT* the same as **D mi 11**

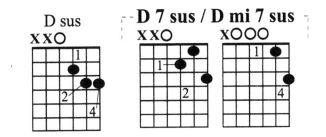

D sus   D 7 sus / D mi 7 sus

G Major Family

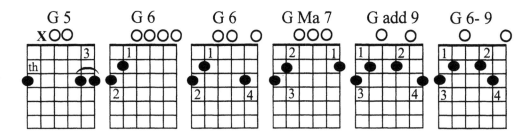

| G 5 | G 6 | G 6 | G Ma 7 | G add 9 | G 6- 9 |

G minor Family

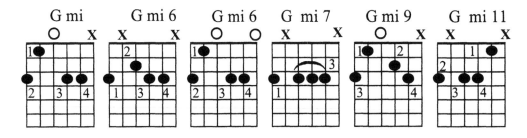

| G mi | G mi 6 | G mi 6 | G mi 7 | G mi 9 | G mi 11 |

G Dominant 7 Family

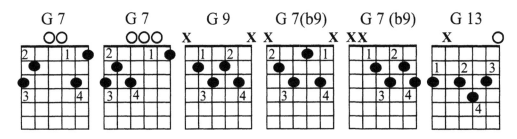

| G 7 | G 7 | G 9 | G 7(b9) | G 7 (b9) | G 13 |

G Suspended Chords

G 7 sus *is the same as* G mi 7 sus
G 11 *is **NOT** the same as* G mi 11

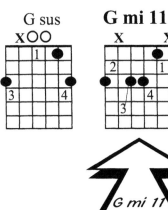

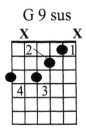

G sus   **G mi 11**   G 9 sus

> If a composer calls for **G mi 11** or **G mi 7 sus,** the **G mi 11** chord at left will do nicely.
> If a composer calls for **G 11** or **G 7 sus,** ***DO NOT USE*** **G mi 11** .

G mi 11 ONLY

Developing a Chord Vocabulary

The chords on the pages labeled "Advanced first position chords" are intended for reference and not immediate memorization- especially if you are a beginner. Think of them the way a chef thinks of a wide spice rack or an artist a box of brilliant pastels. Return to them from time to time for a little inspiration or a fresh idea to bring some zip to that same old stale sounding progression.

With regular review and study, chords that at first seem impossible will eventually become smooth and comfortable. Voicings that sound strange will begin to sound familiar and prove themselves to be useful. Just be patient and give the material a fair chance -it will really pay off!

Beautiful chord progressions and great rhythm guitar are what makes our musical world turn around. The chord maestros of the guitar are responsible for some of the most wonderful music ever made. Great rhythm guitarists are very hard to find -becoming one is an excellent idea.

Suggested listening...

john lennon	*jimi hendrix*	*jim croce*
paul simon	*george van eps*	*keith richards*
tony mottola	*django reinhardt*	*wes montgomery*
joe pass	*jimi page*	*les paul*
chet atkins	*danny gatton*	*ed bickert...*

...Great guitarists renown for their command of chordal playing

Advanced first position chords

C Major Family

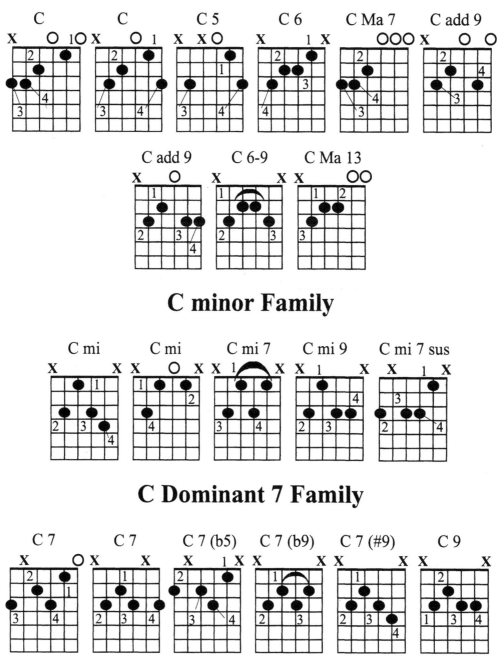

C Suspended Chords

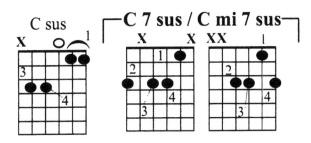

Key: 11th chords and suspended 7th chords.

These 4 types of chords are worthy of a little study:

Dominant Family	minor family
suspended 7th (e.g. C 7 sus)	mi 7th sus (e.g. Cmi 7 sus)
dominant 11th (e.g. C 11)	mi 11th sus (e.g. Cmi 11)

Note the substitution possibilities:

C 7 sus & C 11 substitute for each other -*(both are dominant chords)*
C mi 7 & C mi 11 substitute for each other -*(both are minor chords)*
C 7 sus & C mi 7 sus are interchangeable -*(**unique situation)*
C 11 & C mi 11are <u>NOT</u> interchangeable -*(one dominant, one minor)*

Gray area:

> **C 7 sus is essentially the same chord as C mi 7 sus ****
> **C 7 <u>IS NOT</u> the same chord as C mi 7**

If a composer calls for C 11, he or she wants a **dominant** sound. Don't play a chord you know exclusively as a minor *(e.g. C mi 11).*

If a composer calls for C mi 11 he or she wants a **minor** sound. Don't play a chord you know exclusively as a dominant *(e.g. C 11).*

> ****As an intersting turn of musical theory, **C 7 sus** is identical to **C mi 7 sus**. This is the <u>only time</u> in music where a chord known as a minor chord can be freely substituted for a chord known as a dominant chord. *(For a complete explanation of this, see page 84.)*

Advanced first position chords

F Major Family

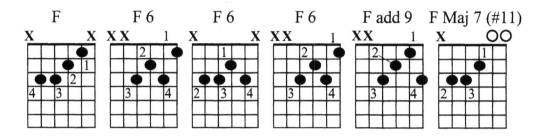

F F 6 F 6 F 6 F add 9 F Maj 7 (#11)

F minor Family

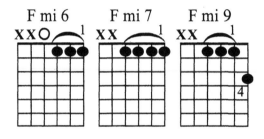

F mi 6 F mi 7 F mi 9

F Dominant 7 Family

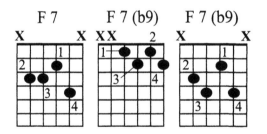

F 7 F 7 (b9) F 7 (b9)

F Suspended Chords

F 7 sus *is the same as* **F mi 7 sus**.....

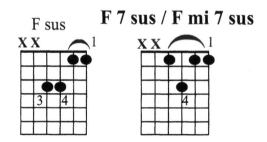

F sus **F 7 sus / F mi 7 sus**

🔑 Since all of the chords in a particular family produce the same **type** of chord sound, they can be used to substitute for each other. This is very good news for anyone who likes to write songs or create unique, individualized arrangements of existing songs. The example below serves to illustrate the principle of chord substitution.

Original Chords:

Possible Substitutes:

D mi Family	G7 Family	C Major Family
D mi 6	G 9	C 6
D mi 7	G 11	C Ma 7
D mi 9	G 13	C Ma 9
D mi 11	G7 (*b*5)	C Ma 13

🔑 If the original chord (the chord you're substituting for) is a **D minor** chord, any chord in the D minor family can be used in its place. For example, **"D mi"** or any chord called **"D mi"** (*e.g. Dmi 7, D mi 9, etc).*

🔑 If the original chord (the chord you're substituting for) is a **C Major** chord, any chord in the C Major family can be used in its place. For example, **"C Ma" "** or any chord called **"C Ma"** (*e.g. C Ma 7. C Ma 13 etc.).* ***(Note: C 6 & C 9/9 are considered Major chords but are rarely, if ever, called C Major 6 or C Major 6/9)***

🔑 If the original chord (the chord you're substituting for) is a **G dominant 7** chord, any chord in the G dominant family can be used in its place. For example, **"G7" "** or any chord called **"G7"** (*e.g.G7, G9, G 13, etc.)* ***(Note: G 6 is generally considered a Major chord <u>not</u> a Dominant chord)***

Key- Essential Guitar Theory

🔑 **Musical Alphabet- A, B, C, D, E, F &G.**
Every note in music has one of these seven names.

🔑 **Flats and Sharps-** Sometimes, two adjacent
notes have another note separating them. These are called
"flats and sharps". Think of as them as the **"black keys"** on a piano.
 Notice how the black keys can have either one of two names. The note
A SHARP is the same as **B FLAT**, **G SHARP** is the same as **A FLAT**.

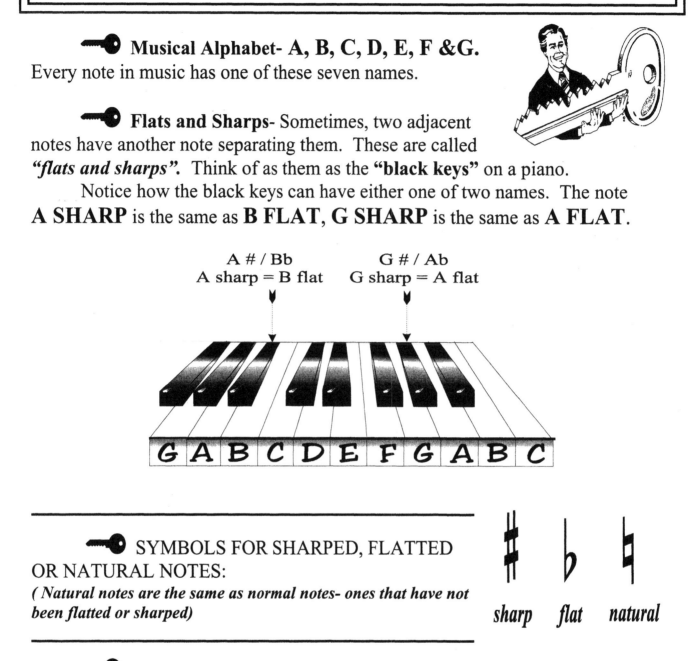

🔑 SYMBOLS FOR SHARPED, FLATTED
OR NATURAL NOTES:
*(Natural notes are the same as normal notes- ones that have not
been flatted or sharped)*

sharp   flat   natural

🔑 **Chromatic Scale** -The name given to __all of the notes__ (flats, sharps
and naturals) when they are played or written for one octave, in order. The
chromatic Scale has 12 notes.

A *A#/Bb* **B C** *C#/Db* **D** *D#/Eb* **E F** *F#/Gb* **G** *G#/Ab* **A**

Important: The notes B & C do not share a flat/sharp note.
The notes E & F do not share a flat/sharp note.

Half Step- Is the name given to a distance of one degree *(one note)* of the chromatic scale. This distance (or *"interval"*) separating any two adjacent notes is called a **HALF STEP**. For example, from **F# to G** or from **C# to D** as illustrated below.

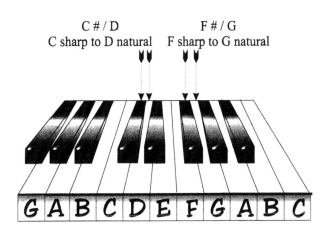

Whole Step- The name given to a distance of two degrees *(two notes)* of the chromatic scale. This distance, or **interval**, of two half steps is called a **WHOLE STEP**. For example, from **G to A** or from **F# to G#** as illustrated below.

Octave-Two notes separated by 12 degrees *(half steps)* of the chromatic scale have the same name. One of the notes is exactly twice as high in pitch as the other note. These two notes are said to be *an octave apart*.

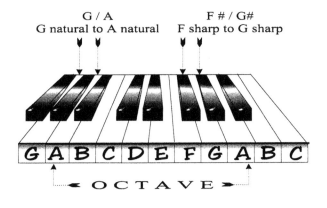

On the guitar, all the frets are separated by a distance of a **half step**. Each fret is equal to one note *(degree)* of the chromatic scale.

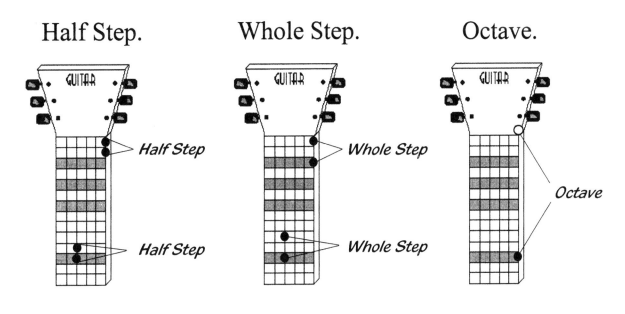

—o Every single note on the guitar can be given a letter name taken from the *chromatic scale*:

A *A#/Bb* **B C** *C#/Db* **D** *D#/Eb* **E F** *F#/Gb* **G** *G#/Ab* **A**

—o The open strings, for example, have the following names:

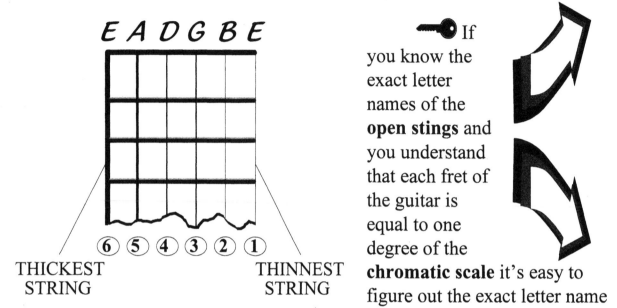

THICKEST STRING

THINNEST STRING

—o If you know the exact letter names of the **open stings** and you understand that each fret of the guitar is equal to one degree of the **chromatic scale** it's easy to figure out the exact letter name of any note on your guitar as pictured on page 21.

—o In order to really play and understand the Pop, Rock and Blues guitar you must know the **exact letter name** of each and every note on *string six* and *string five*.

Review:

Discuss the following with a friend or teacher:

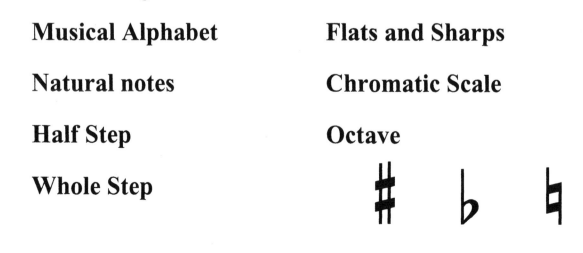

Musical Alphabet	**Flats and Sharps**
Natural notes	**Chromatic Scale**
Half Step	**Octave**
Whole Step	

String six
Low "E"

String five
Low "A"

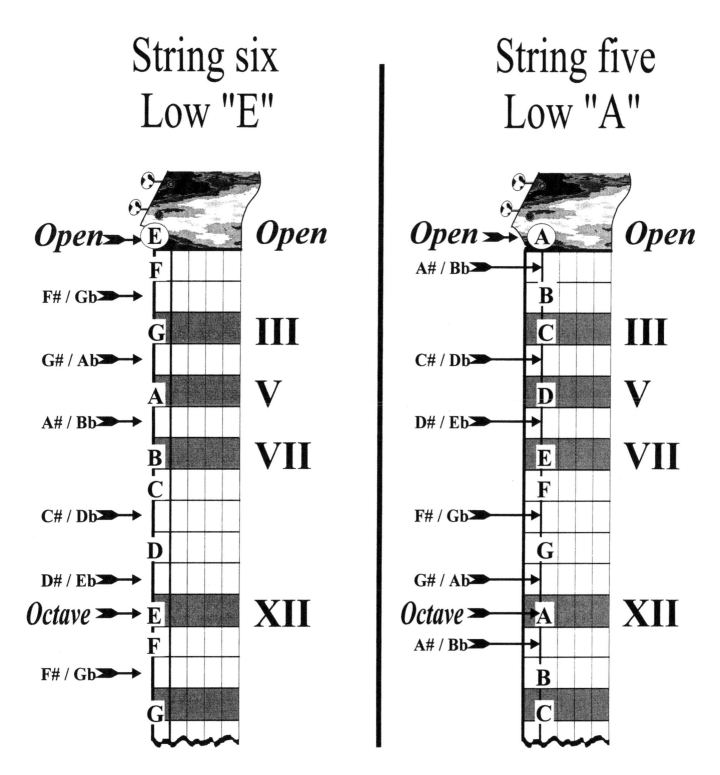

The name of an open string and the name of the note on the 12th fret of that string are exactly the same- only an octave apart.

Notice the large roman numerals (**III, V, VII** and **XII**). These are the frets that have position markers ("dots") on most guitars. Memorize the names of those notes first (on frets **III, V, VII** and **XII**) and use them as reference points while playing and practicing.

Call frets **III, V, VII** and **XII** the *LANDMARKS*.

Root 6 & Root 5 Thinking.

The system of guitaristic thinking presented in this book revolves around memorizing the names of the notes on strings 6 and 5. This is *absolutely critical.* I've suggested using a system of *LANDMARKS* which correspond to the position markers *("dots")* found on frets **III, V, VII**, and **XII** on most guitars .

The shadings on our guitar neck diagrams reflect the frets which are thought of as landmarks.
(frets III, V, VII, and XII)

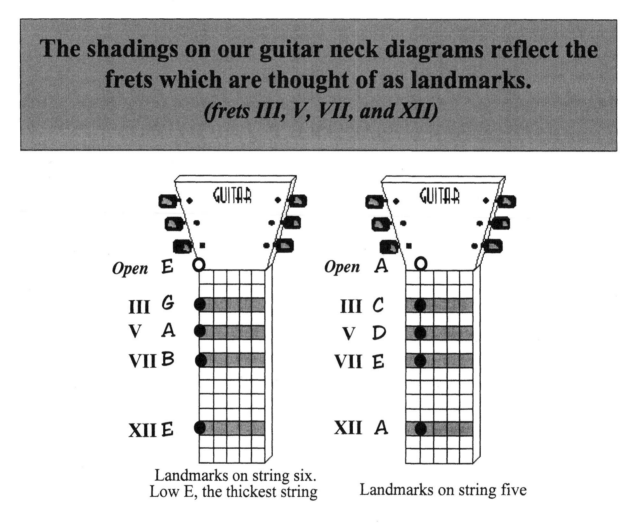

Landmarks on string six.
Low E, the thickest string

Landmarks on string five

Each and every note in the chromatic scale,

A *A#/Bb* **B** **C** *C#/Db* **D** *D#/Eb* **E** **F** *F#/Gb* **G** *G#/Ab* **A**

is important in the playing of and thinking about music. The exercises on the opposite page will help you to develop the **crucial ability** to quickly name any note on the two thickest strings- low "E" and low "A". Write in the note names in the space above each guitar neck and check your work against the answers on the bottom of the page.

Note Naming Exercise

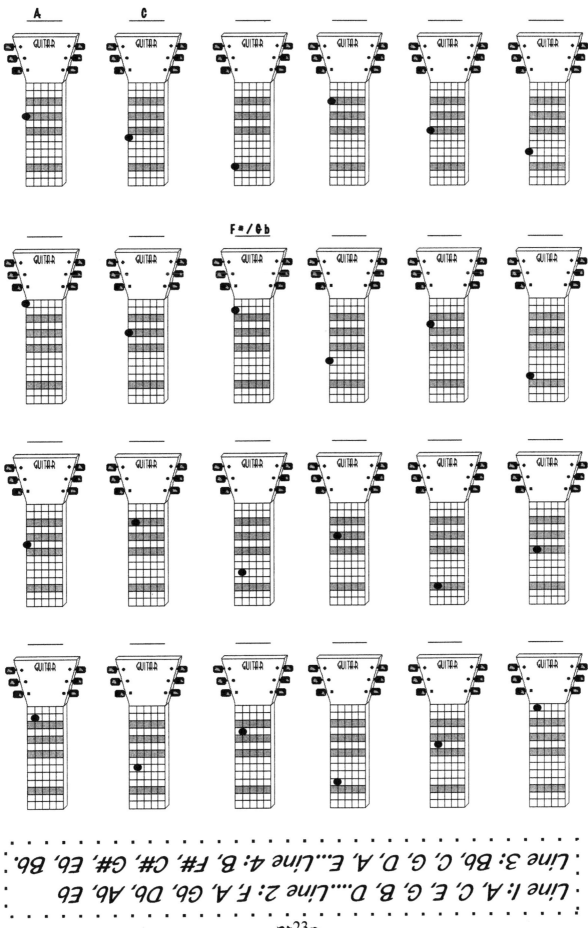

Barre Chords

Barre *(or "Bar")* chords have several notes played on the **same fret** by the **same straight finger**. In guitar books and magazines, the diagram indicating the use of a **barre chord** is a thick curved line connecting several notes on the same fret as seen in the illustrations below.

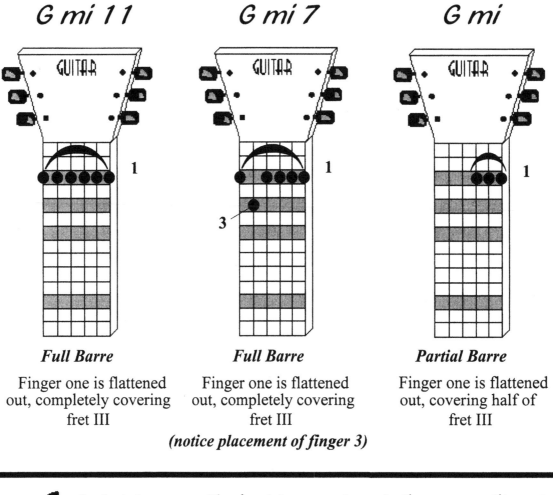

G mi 11

Full Barre

Finger one is flattened out, completely covering fret III

G mi 7

Full Barre

Finger one is flattened out, completely covering fret III

(notice placement of finger 3)

G mi

Partial Barre

Finger one is flattened out, covering half of fret III

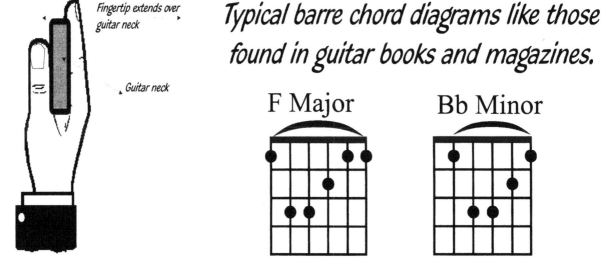

Fingertip extends over guitar neck

Guitar neck

Typical barre chord diagrams like those found in guitar books and magazines.

F Major

Bb Minor

Developing a Barre Chord

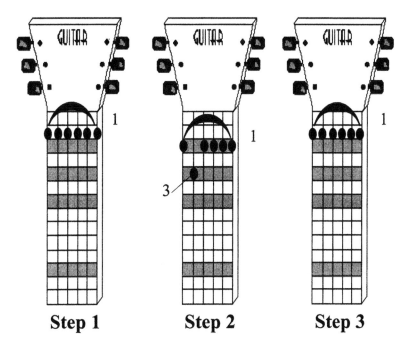

Step 1   **Step 2**   **Step 3**

The exercise illustrated at left is an excellent way to develop *the touch* needed for a good barre chord. Most students are under the false impression that a tremendous amount of strength is needed to play the barre chord. This is not entirely true *(unless your guitar is a "junker"!)*. The ability to play barre chords is a matter of **touch, finesse, practice** and **patience**.

Step 1- Place a firm, straight first finger over the entirety of fret II as shown in the illustration above. At this point, your finger is **completely straight** and at a *90 degree angle* with the ground *(pointing at the ceiling)*. Slowly strum your guitar while listening for **SIX CLEAR NOTES**.

Step 2- Place a firm, straight first finger over the entirety of fret III. Place the *__ARCHED__* **tip of your curved third finger** directly on top of string five, fret five. Slowly strum your guitar so that you hear **SIX CLEAR NOTES**. Notice that finger one is still *pointing at the ceiling.*

Step 3- Place a straight finger 1 over the entirety of fret II as shown in the illustration above. At this point, your finger is completely straight and at a *90 degree angle* with the ground. Slowly strum your guitar so that you again hear **SIX CLEAR NOTES**.

Repeat this exercise on every possible fret:
Move slowly & smoothly up the neck of your guitar one fret at a time.

When seen in a standard chord graph, each chord on the guitar has a shape to it. The open string chords of

E Major   A Major

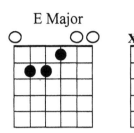

E Major and **A major** are particularly important because they are at the core of a critical concept: *Movable Chords*.

If each and every note in one of these chords were raised in pitch by the *exact same fret distance,* the result would be an entirely new chord with the **same quality** but a **different name**. These are called *Movable Chords.*

➤ *Moving a Root 6 Chord:*

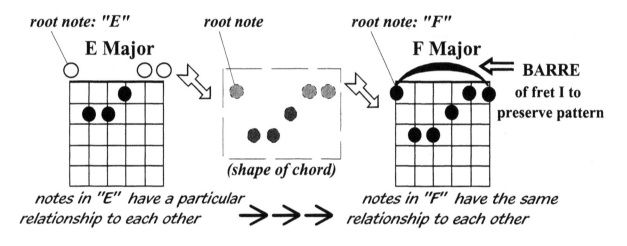

root note: "E"   root note   root note: "F"

E Major   **F Major**

← **BARRE** of fret I to preserve pattern

(shape of chord)

notes in "E" have a particular relationship to each other   →→→   *notes in "F" have the same relationship to each other*

The root note of a basic **E Major chord** is on string six. Therefore, we know that a chord with this particular shape derives its name from the note on string six. When the *entire shape* of an **"E"** chord is moved **up in pitch** by one fret, the resulting chord must now be an **F Major chord**. This is because the name of the note being played on string six is now **"F"**. At this point, the exact letter names of the other five notes are **not important**. What *is* important is seeing beauty and simplicity in the concept of movable chord shapes.

The same chord shape that moves from one spot on the neck to another is called a *movable chord.* In the diagram above, all the notes of an **E Major** have been moved up in pitch by precisely one fret. The result is an **F Major Chord**. The **E Major** chord has the same shape as the **F Major** chord. Both chords are called:

ROOT SIX MOVABLE CHORDS.

⚯ *Moving a Root 5 chord:*

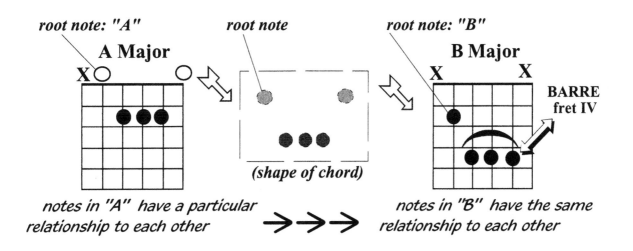

root note: "A"

A Major

root note

root note: "B"

B Major

BARRE
fret IV

(shape of chord)

notes in "A" have a particular
relationship to each other

→ → →

notes in "B" have the same
relationship to each other

The same principles hold true for **A Major** in position I *-a root five chord*. The chord derives its name from its fifth string root note.

The name of the note located on fret II, string five, is **"B"**. It stands to reason, then, that when an **"A"** chord shape is played on fret II, a **B Major chord** results. Both chords are called

ROOT FIVE MOVABLE CHORDS.

⚯ *Moving Root 6 & Root 5 chords in relation to the system of landmarks:*

The methods described for ascertaining the exact letter name of any note on **string 6** and **string 5** are essential for giving names to movable chords.

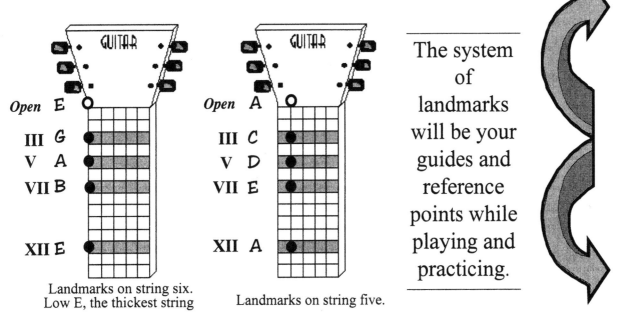

Open E

III G
V A
VII B

XII E

Landmarks on string six.
Low E, the thickest string

Open A

III C
V D
VII E

XII A

Landmarks on string five.

The system
of
landmarks
will be your
guides and
reference
points while
playing and
practicing.

Fingerings of conventional Root 6 Bar Chords

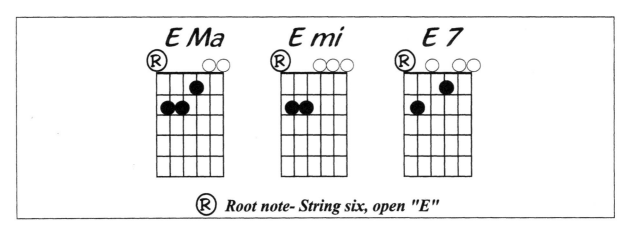

® *Root note- String six, open "E"*

Parent Chords: Above are the three ***Root 6*** chord shapes in widespread use by all guitarists. I call them ***"parent chords"*** since they are the basis for some of the most common chords in the world of guitar playing.

      Transfer these chords to any spot on the neck with the use of a first finger barre and the fingerings below.

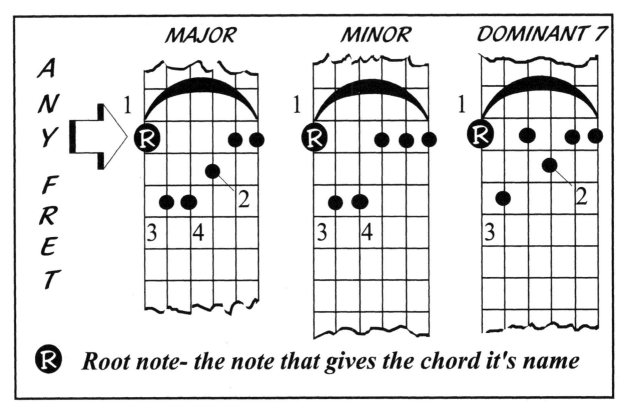

® *Root note- the note that gives the chord it's name*

NOTES: The chord forms and fingerings illustrated above are the heart of Pop/Rock and Blues guitar technique. Note the words ***"ANY FRET"*** in the above diagram. This means that these chords are playable anywhere on the neck. The name of the note on String 6 (**®**) is the Root note and determines the name of the chord.

      On the opposite page, the ***root 6 movable chords*** are illustrated in reference to the landmarks on string six. The chromatic scale and the landmarks are the keys to learning barre chords.

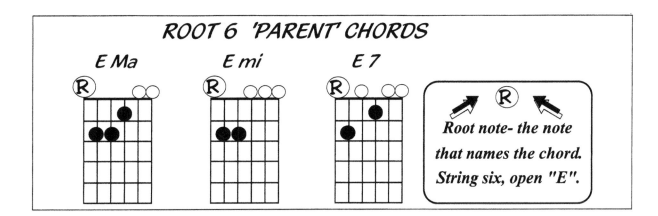

ROOT 6 'PARENT' CHORDS

E Ma   E mi   E 7

Root note- the note that names the chord. String six, open "E".

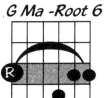
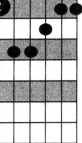
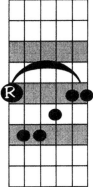

G Ma -Root 6   G mi -Root 6   G 7 -Root 6

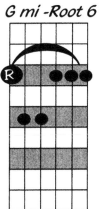
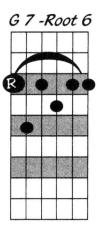

A Ma -Root 6   A mi -Root 6   A 7 -Root 6

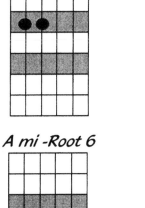
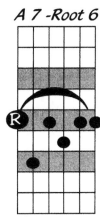

B Ma -Root 6   B mi -Root 6   B 7 -Root 6

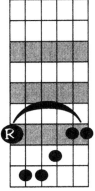
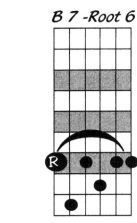

Root Note- located on STRING SIX, is the note that names the chord.

Fingerings of conventional Root 5 Bar Chords

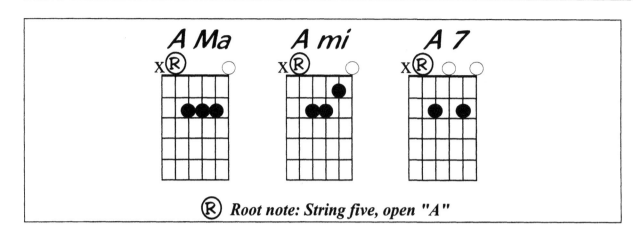

The shapes of the three **"parent chords"** above are transferable to any spot on the neck with the use of a first finger barre. Below are the most widely used fingerings for these ever popular chords.

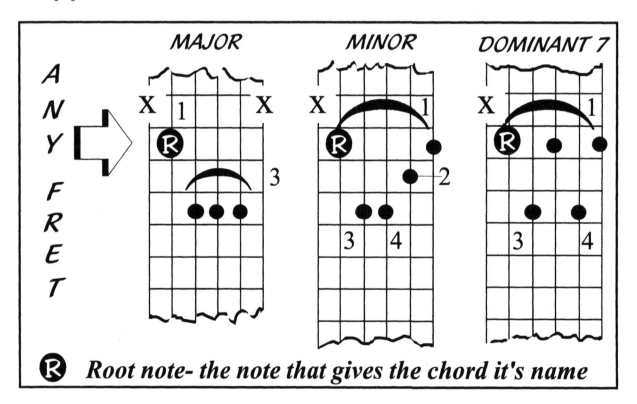

NOTES: The barre chords diagrammed above are equally as important as the root six chords *Notice the "X's" indicating dead strings.* To play a root five **Major** chord, you must barre with the third finger while fretting the root note with the first finger. This is one of the most difficult barre chords. Of course, the positions of the wrist and elbow are critical to playing a Root 5 Major chord -experiment.

The words *"ANY FRET"* signify that these chords are playable anywhere on the neck. On the opposite page, the ***root 5 movable chords*** are illustrated in reference to the landmarks on string five. The secrets to mastering barre chords are a thorough understanding of the chromatic scale and the landmarks.

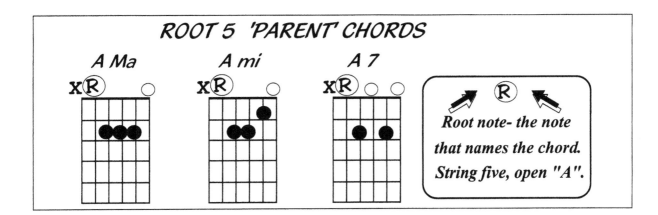

ROOT 5 'PARENT' CHORDS

A Ma   A mi   A 7

Root note- the note that names the chord. String five, open "A".

C Ma- Root 5   C mi- Root 5   C 7- Root 5

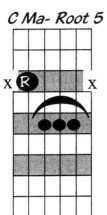 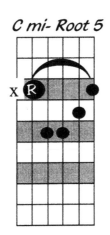 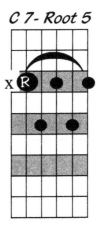

D Ma- Root 5   D mi- Root 5   D 7- Root 5

  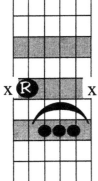 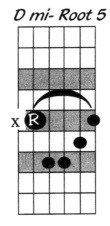 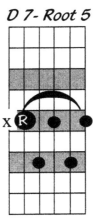

E Ma- Root 5   E mi- Root 5   E 7- Root 5

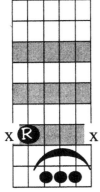 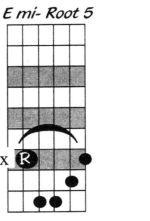 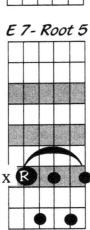

Root Note -located on STRING FIVE, is the note that names the chord.

~31~

Mastering & Moving Root Six Barre Chords.

Open String:
LANDMARK.

Any note in the chromatic scale can be the root note of any type of chord -Major, minor or dominant.

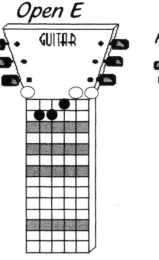

Open E

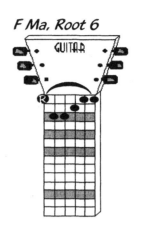

F Ma, Root 6

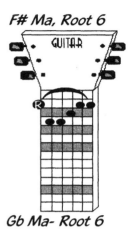

F# Ma, Root 6

Gb Ma- Root 6

Fret III:
LANDMARK.

Knowing the name of every note on string six means assures your playing and understanding Barre chords.

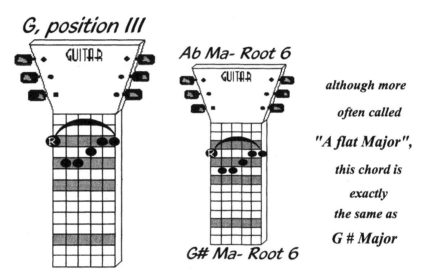

G, position III

Ab Ma- Root 6

although more often called "A flat Major", this chord is exactly the same as G # Major

G# Ma- Root 6

Fret V:
LANDMARK.

Any note on string six can be the root note of any type of chord.

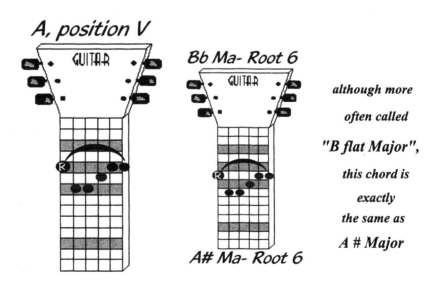

A, position V

Bb Ma- Root 6

although more often called "B flat Major", this chord is exactly the same as A # Major

A# Ma- Root 6

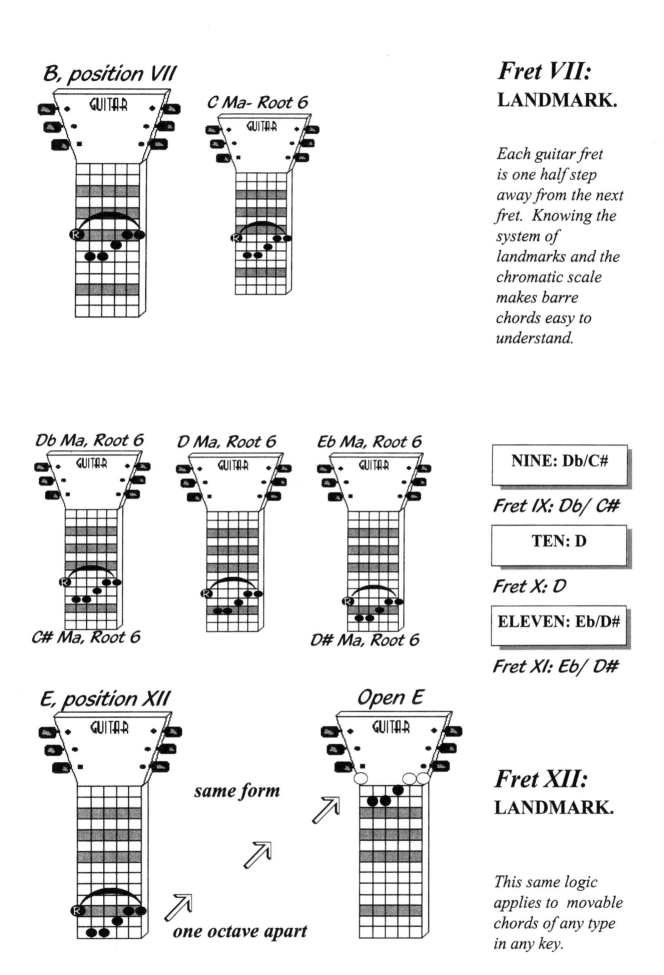

B, position VII

GUITAR

C Ma- Root 6

GUITAR

Fret VII:
LANDMARK.

Each guitar fret is one half step away from the next fret. Knowing the system of landmarks and the chromatic scale makes barre chords easy to understand.

Db Ma, Root 6

GUITAR

D Ma, Root 6

GUITAR

Eb Ma, Root 6

GUITAR

C# Ma, Root 6

D# Ma, Root 6

NINE: Db/C#

Fret IX: Db/ C#

TEN: D

Fret X: D

ELEVEN: Eb/D#

Fret XI: Eb/ D#

E, position XII

GUITAR

same form

Open E

GUITAR

one octave apart

Fret XII:
LANDMARK.

This same logic applies to movable chords of any type in any key.

~33~

Name that Root

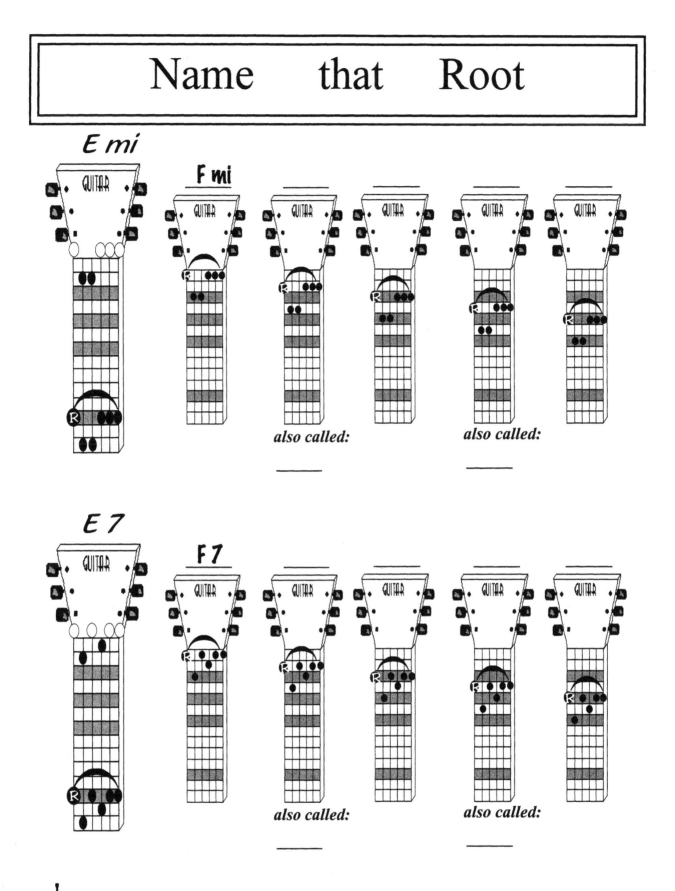

E mi

F mi

also called:
___

also called:
___

E 7

F 7

also called:
___

also called:
___

🎸Use a pencil to fill in the blanks. *(answers on the opposite page)*

🎸Play **and name** all the chords on this page and on page 35.

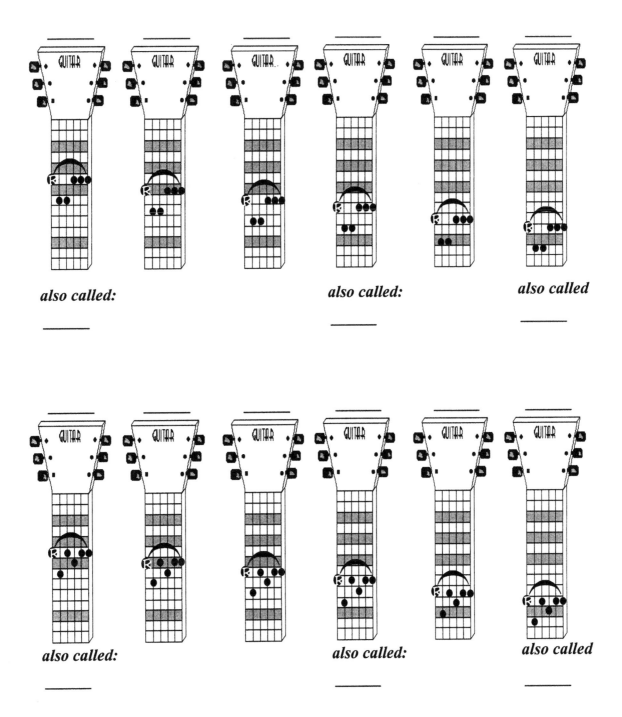

also called: _____

also called: _____

also called _____

_____

also called: _____

also called: _____

also called _____

_____

Follow the chromatic scale: Top line- Fmi, F#mi, Gmi, G#mi, Ami, Bbmi, Bmi, Cmi, C#mi, Dmi, D#mi. Bottom line-F7, F#7, G7, G#7, A7, Bb7, B7, C7, C#7, D7, D#7. Follows the chromatic scale.

Mastering & Moving Root Five Barre Chords.

Open String: LANDMARK.

Any note in the chromatic scale can be the root note of any type of chord -Major, minor or dominant.

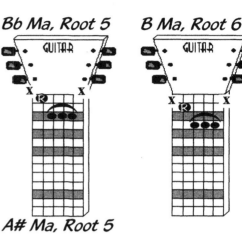

Open A

Bb Ma, Root 5

A# Ma, Root 5

B Ma, Root 6

Fret III: LANDMARK.

Knowing the name of every note on string five means that you can play any type of chord.

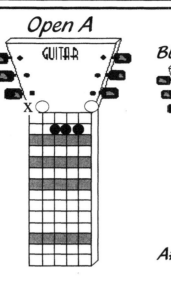

C, position III

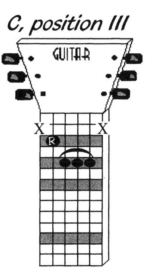

Db Ma, Root 5

C# Ma, Root 6

although more often called "D flat Major" this chord is exactly the same as C # Major

Fret V: LANDMARK.

Play and name all the chords pictured on this and page 37.

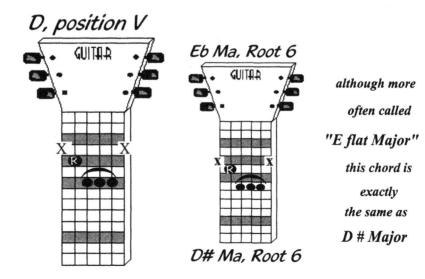

D, position V

Eb Ma, Root 6

D# Ma, Root 6

although more often called "E flat Major" this chord is exactly the same as D # Major

E, position VII

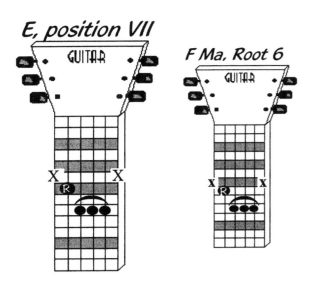

F Ma. Root 6

Fret VII:
LANDMARK.

Each guitar fret is one half step away from the next fret. Knowing the system of landmarks and the chromatic scale makes barre chords easy.

Gb Ma, Root 5

G Ma, Root 5

Ab Ma, Root 5

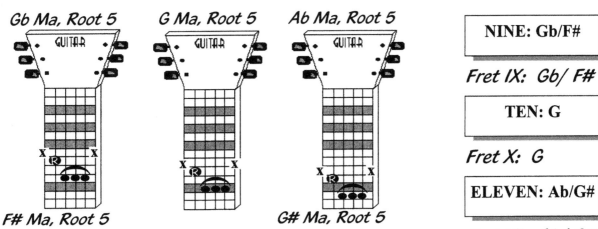

F# Ma, Root 5

G# Ma, Root 5

NINE: Gb/F#

Fret IX: Gb/ F#

TEN: G

Fret X: G

ELEVEN: Ab/G#

Fret XI: Ab/ G#

A, position XII

Open A

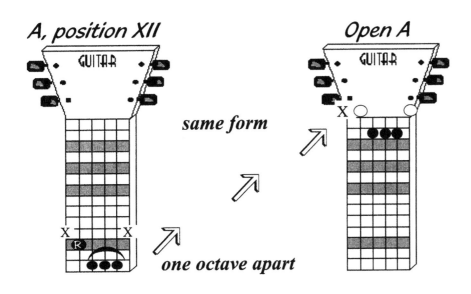

same form

one octave apart

Fret XII:
LANDMARK.

This same logic applies to movable chords of any type in any key.

Name that Root

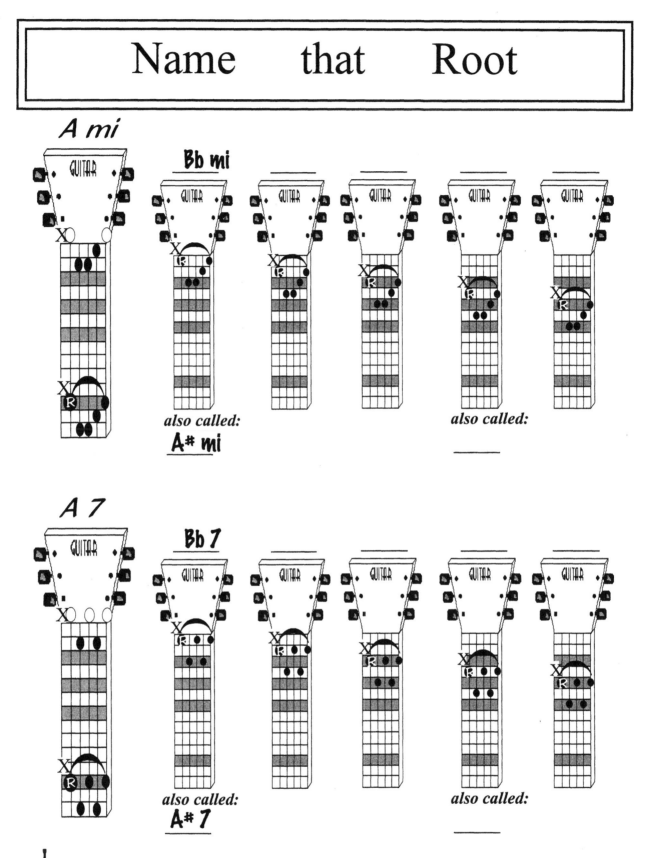

A mi

Bb mi

also called:
A# mi

also called:
_____

A 7

Bb 7

also called:
A# 7

also called:
_____

Use a pencil to fill in the blanks. *(answers on the opposite page)*

Play **and name** all the chords on this page and on page 39.

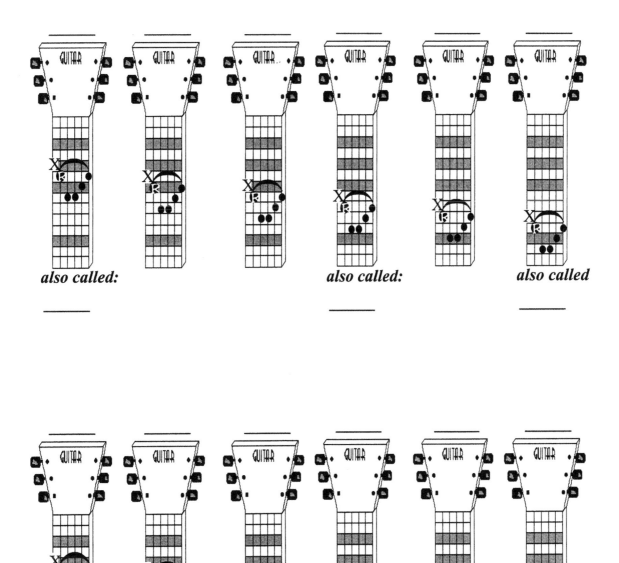

also called: _____

also called: _____

also called _____

also called: _____

also called: _____

also called: _____

Follow the chromatic scale: Top line- Bbmi, Bmi, Cmi, C#mi, Dmi, D#mi, Emi, Fmi, F#mi, Gmi, G#mi. • Bottom line- Bb7, B7, C7, C#7, D7, D#7, E7, F7, F#7, G7, G#7. • Follows the chromatic scale.

Alternate Voicings.

Here are 2 versions of an E Major chord. Play them over & over.

E Major, Root 6   **E Major, Root 5**

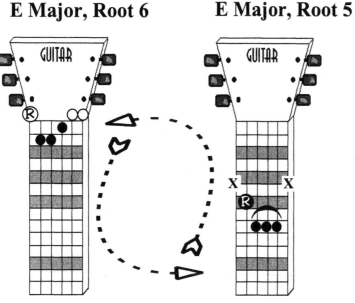

As you play these two chords, notice that they produce the same overall musical effect.

If someone were to say *"Play an E Major chord,"* either of these two versions *('voicings')* would be totally acceptable. There **are** some differences between the two E Major chords. Your musical tastes will tell you which one is the correct chord for a particular situation.

Here are 2 versions of an A Major chord. Play them over & over.

A Major, Root 5   **A Major, Root 6**

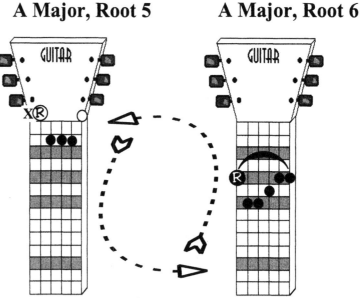

The same thing applies to the two voicings of the A Major chord. In a song that calls for an A Major sound, either one is perfectly fine.

For any guitar chord, there are at least two *voicings:* a Root 6 chord and a Root 5 chord.

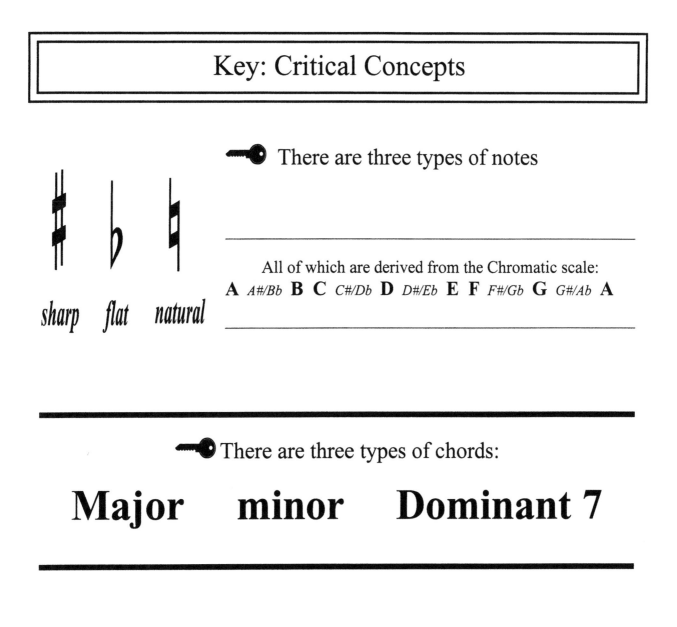

There are three types of notes

sharp   flat   natural

All of which are derived from the Chromatic scale:
A *A#/Bb* **B C** *C#/Db* **D** *D#/Eb* **E F** *F#/Gb* **G** *G#/Ab* **A**

There are three types of chords:

Major   minor   Dominant 7

Any note in the chromatic scale *(sharp, flat or natural)* can be the root note of any type of chord:

For Example:

A # mi, A # Ma, A # 7
B *b* mi, B *b* Ma, B *b* 7, C # mi, C # Ma, C # 7, D *b* mi, D *b* Ma, D *b* 7,
D # mi, D # Ma, D # 7, E b mi, E b Ma, E b 7, F # mi, F # Ma, F # 7,
G *b* mi, G *b* Ma, G *b* 7, G # mi, G # Ma, G # 7, A *b* mi, A *b* Ma, A *b* 7....

Are all possible chord names. Play the Root 6 and Root 5 versions for each one of them.

There are two *"automatic"* voicings for any guitar chord you may want to play: **A Root six version** and a **Root five version**. The two versions, or *"voicings"*, of any particular chord have the same basic sound as each other and produce the same overall musical effect: they can be used interchangeably.

Example 1: G Major, G minor and G 7: *(two versions each)*

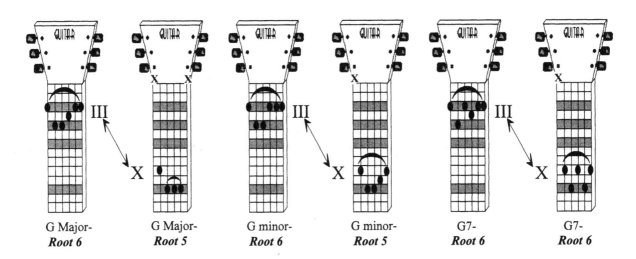

| G Major-
Root 6 | G Major-
Root 5 | G minor-
Root 6 | G minor-
Root 5 | G7-
Root 6 | G7-
Root 6 |

Example 2: F Major, F minor and F 7: *(two versions each)*

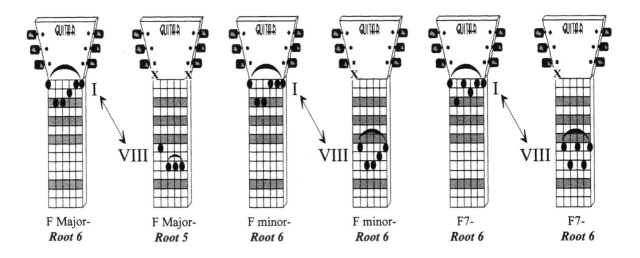

| F Major-
Root 6 | F Major-
Root 5 | F minor-
Root 6 | F minor-
Root 6 | F7-
Root 6 | F7-
Root 6 |

Practice and play these chords slowly, smoothly, and with a beat. Make seamless transitions from one clean, free-ringing chord to the next chord.

BARRE CHORD EXERCISE

‖: ♩ ♩ ♩ ♩ ♩ ♩ :‖

⑥ **⑤** **⑥** **⑤** **⑥** **⑤**

or... ⑤ ⑥ ⑤ ⑥ ⑤ ⑥

C	C	C-	C-	C7	C7
G	G	G-	G-	G7	G7
D	D	D-	D-	D7	D7
A	A	A-	A-	A7	A7
E	E	E-	E-	E7	E7
B	B	B-	B-	B7	B7
F#	F#	F#-	F#-	F#7	F#7
Gb	Gb	Gb-	Gb-	Gb7	Gb7
Db	Db	Db-	Db-	Db7	Db7

Play this exercise exactly like examples 1 & 2 on the opposite page.

🎸 Turn on your metronome.

🎸 Start by strumming a **Root 6 "C" Major**, letting it ring out for two beats.

🎸 Repeat this process using the root notes G, D, A, E, A, B, F#, Gb, & Db.

🎸 Try playing first a Root 5 chord and then a Root 6 chord for each line.

⬉

Play these exercise exactly like examples 1 & 2 on the opposite page.

BARRE CHORD EXERCISE II

Play this exercise exactly as shown on page 43.

6 **5** **6** **5** **6** **5**

or... 5 6 5 6 5 6

Turn on your metronome.

Start by strumming a **Root 6 "F" Major**, letting it ring out for two beats.

This entire page must be completed with a solid, flowing beat. Play the exercises slowly.

F	F	F-	F-	F7	F7
Bb	Bb	Bb-	Bb-	Bb7	Bb7
Eb	Eb	Eb-	Eb-	Eb7	Eb7
Ab	Ab	Ab-	Ab-	Ab7	Ab7
C#	C#	C#-	C#-	C#7	C#7
G#	G#	G#-	G#-	G#7	G#7
D#	D#	D#-	D#-	D#7	D#7
A#	A#	A#-	A#-	A#7	A#7

Play these exercises exactly like those on page 43. When these two pages can be completed with no trouble, you know barre chords.

Music Theory: The Major Scale

The basis and foundation of music theory is the Major scale. The well known *sound* of the Major scale is that of **" Do Re Mi Fa Sol La Ti Do"**. All discussions of music theory are ultimately based on the Major scale.

Any of the scales in music derive their particular sounds from the distances separating their notes. This is called a *scale formula.* The chromatic scale *(see page 18)*, for example, has a distance of a half step between each one of its notes.

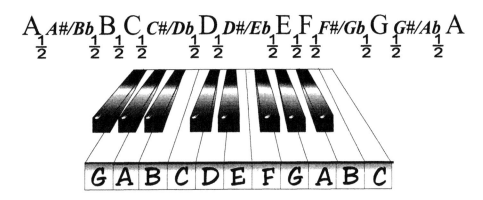

The formula for the chromatic scale is expressed as:
" half, half, half, half, half, half, half, half, half, half, half, half "

The formula for a Major scale is expressed as:
" whole, whole, half, whole, whole, whole, half "

The Major scale can be beautifully illustrated on one string of the guitar...

...or by playing only the white keys on a keyboard beginning and ending with "C".

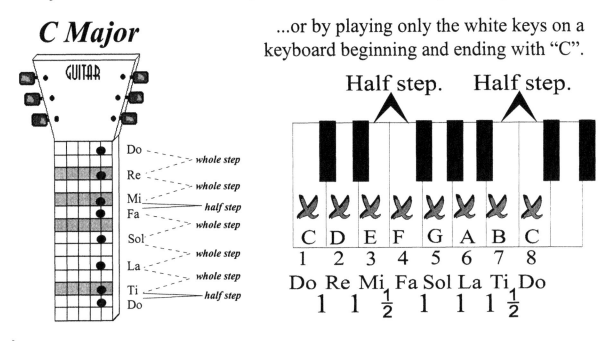

The formula for the major Scale is expressed as
"whole, whole, half, whole, whole, whole, half".

Any note in the chromatic scale can be the root of its own Major scale. It's possible to build twelve (and only twelve) separate and distinct Major Scales using the notes of the chromatic scale. Each new and unique Major scale is said to be a *"new key"*. There are twelve separate and distinct Major Scales and therefore **twelve keys** in the language of music.

Every 8 note major scale contains all seven letters of the musical alphabet with the first *(and last)* note of the scale being the **root note**. In order to play *(and hear)* a Major Scale starting on the "G", note we would first need the letters **"G A B C D E F G"**. According to the Scale formula the interval separating the last two notes must be a half step. That being the case, the type of "F" note we use must be an **"F#"**, not an **"F"**.

> The correct *spelling* of a G Major scale is:
> # G A B C D E F# G

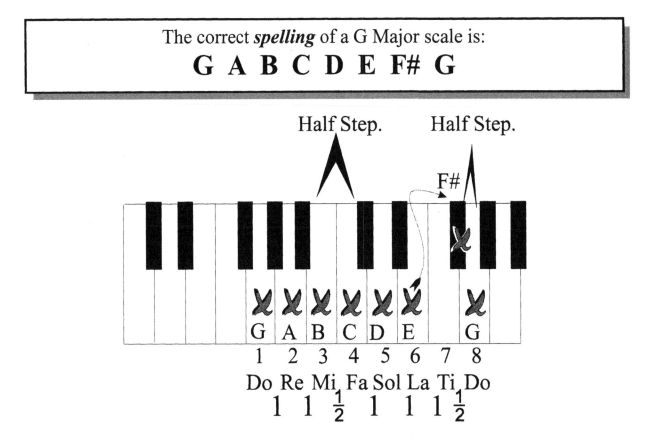

There is a demand for "F#" instead of "F natural" to preserve the formula *and sound* of the Major Scale. If you construct a major Scale with a root note of "G", there is one sharp needed **(F#)** in order to make it come out with the right sound. This is what is meant by the following statement:

"The key of G Major has one sharp"

To construct a Major scale with a root note of "D", we first need to have these notes:

D E F G A B C D.

The *Major Scale formula* states that the interval separating notes **3&4** and also notes **7&8** must be a half step. That being the case, the type of "F" note we must use is **"F sharp"** and not **"F natural"**. Accordingly, type of "C" note we use is **"C Sharp"**, not **"C natural".**

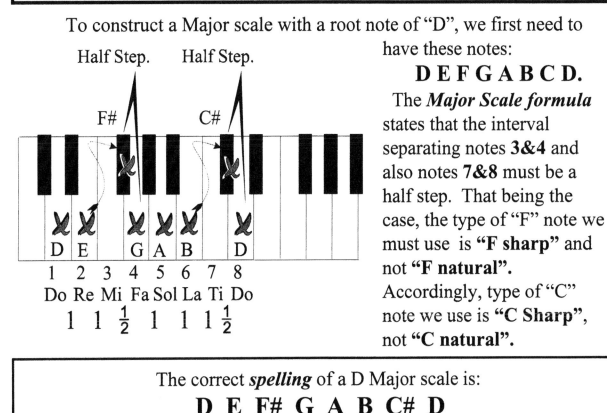

The correct *spelling* of a D Major scale is:
D E F# G A B C# D

Each new Major scale we construct is the basis of its own system of playing and composing called a *Key*.

The two keys we have studied so far *(the key of "D Major" & the key of "G Major")* are called **sharp keys** because they need to use sharped notes to have the correct formula *-and therefore sound* of their own, individual Major scale.

Flat Keys

Some keys need to use flatted notes to have the correct formula and sound of their own Major scale. They key of "F Major" is an example of a *flat key*.

To construct an F Major scale, we must start and end with a note of "F" and have every other letter of the musical alphabet represented once: **F G A B C D E F.** If the interval separating A & B (notes 3&4) must be a half step, the **"B"** note must then be flatted *(Bb).* It's incorrect to call this note **"A#"** because a note named **"A"** is alreday included in the spelling.

The correct *spelling* of the F Major scale is:
F G A Bb C D E F

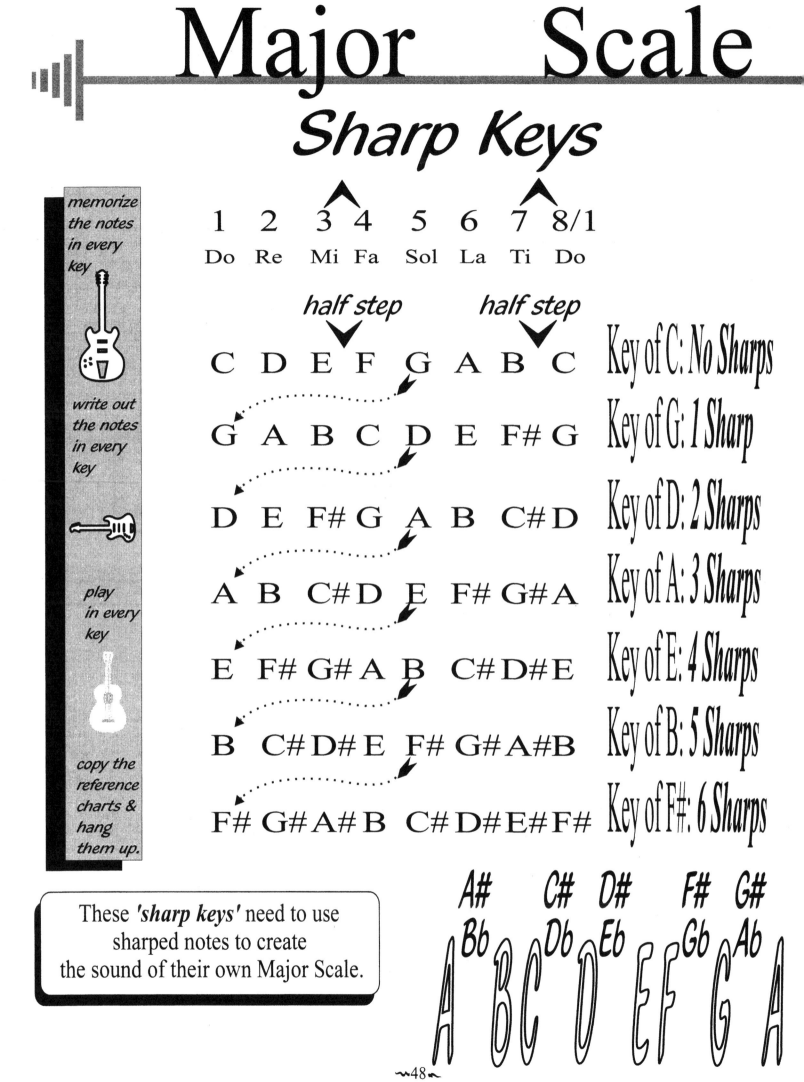

Major Scale

Sharp Keys

memorize the notes in every key

write out the notes in every key

play in every key

copy the reference charts & hang them up.

```
        ^                    ^
1   2   3   4   5   6   7   8/1
Do  Re  Mi  Fa  Sol La  Ti  Do
```

```
      half step        half step
         ∨                 ∨
C   D   E   F   G   A   B   C      Key of C: No Sharps

G   A   B   C   D   E   F#  G      Key of G: 1 Sharp

D   E   F#  G   A   B   C#  D      Key of D: 2 Sharps

A   B   C#  D   E   F#  G#  A      Key of A: 3 Sharps

E   F#  G#  A   B   C#  D#  E      Key of E: 4 Sharps

B   C#  D#  E   F#  G#  A#  B      Key of B: 5 Sharps

F#  G#  A#  B   C#  D#  E#  F#     Key of F#: 6 Sharps
```

These **'sharp keys'** need to use sharped notes to create the sound of their own Major Scale.

```
    A#      C#  D#        F#  G#
    Bb      Db  Eb        Gb  Ab
A  B   C   D   E  F   G   A
```

Reference Charts

Flat Keys

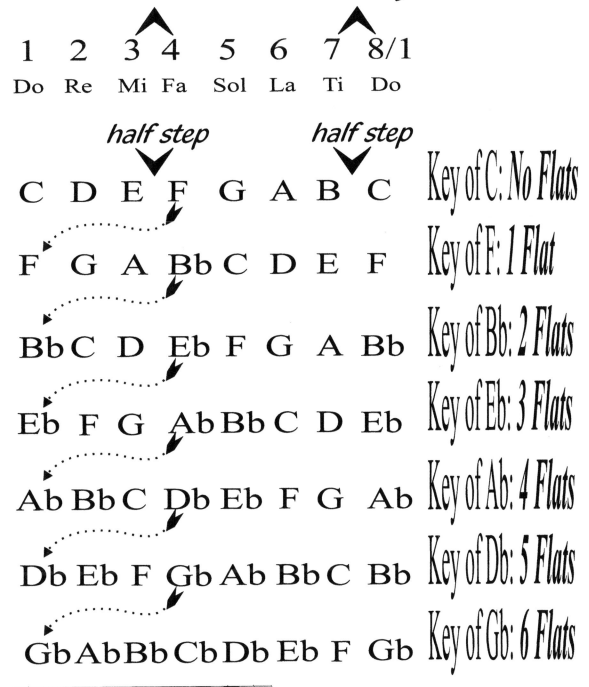

Key of C: *No Flats*

Key of F: *1 Flat*

Key of Bb: *2 Flats*

Key of Eb: *3 Flats*

Key of Ab: *4 Flats*

Key of Db: *5 Flats*

Key of Gb: *6 Flats*

Play a Major scale in every key

write in every key

practice in every key

memorize these charts

These *'flat keys'* need to use flatted notes to create the sound of their own Major Scale.

Key: The Circle of Fifths

The diagram on the opposite page is **the** classic method of organizing the 12 keys in the language of Music. The inherent logic of this circle is very clearly evident when studying the two preceding pages of this book ('sharp keys' & 'flat keys').

When moving clockwise around the *circle of fifths*, the keys are separated by an *interval of a fifth*. That is to say "G" is the fifth note of a "C" Major scale while "D" is the fifth note of a "G" Major scale. I have clearly diagrammed this on page 48, entitled 'sharp keys'. When the keys are organized in this manner, each successive key contains **one more sharp** than the previous key. This is the logic and beauty of the *circle of fifths*.

When moving counter clockwise, the diagram is often called the *circle of fourths*. In this case, each new key contains **one more flat** than the previous key. The keys are separated by an interval of a fourth. This means "F" is the fourth note of a "C" Major scale while "Bb" is the fourth note of an "F" Major scale and so on. I've illustrated this idea on the page 49, entitled 'flat keys'.

The circle of fifths is a systematic approach to organizing and memorizing the 12 keys of music according to the number of flats or sharps a key contains. All musicians must be totally comfortable with the circle of fifths.

E sharp & C flat

E sharp is another way of saying **F natural**. **C flat** is another way of saying **B natural**. These are called *enharmonic notes*.

The key of **F sharp** must contain a seventh note one half step lower than "F#". Obviously this can't be called "F" because that would mean the scale could not be written correctly- the scale would have two types of "F" notes, *F sharp and F natural*. Therefore we must call the seventh note of an **F Sharp Major** scale "E#".

The key of **G Flat** must contain a fourth note one half step higher than "Bb". Obviously this can't be called "B" because that would mean **this** scale could not be written correctly- the scale would have two types of "B" notes, *B flat and B natural*. Therefore we must call the fourth note of a **G Flat Major** scale "Cb".

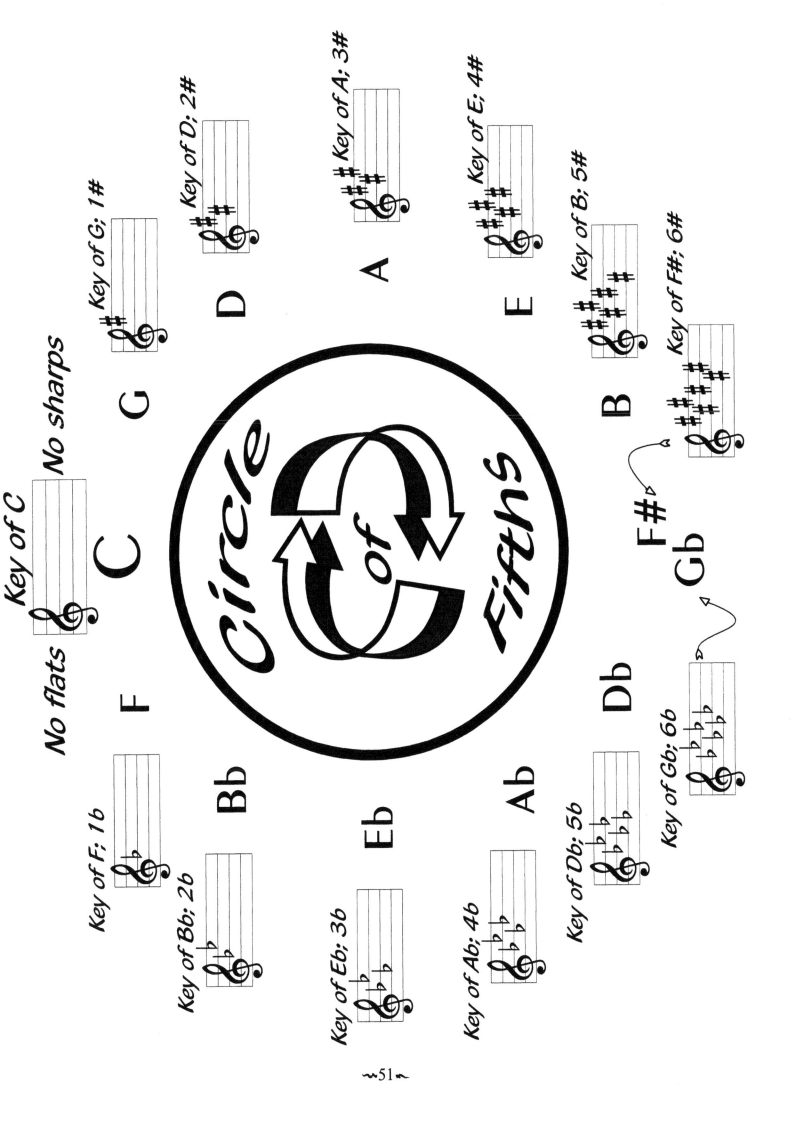

Advanced Movable Chords.

Serious guitarists have a terrific interest in playing all types of chords, not just the 'plain old' **Major, minor and Dominant 7** forms we've mastered so far. Tempting as it might be, let's **not** think of advanced chords as *"Jazz chords"*. The chords of the **7th, 9th, 11th & 13th** varieties are very useful in all types of music- *not just jazz*.

As you develop your chord vocabulary, keep two things in mind:

1.) The root note of each chord and how to **transpose** *(change key to)* it. Any movable chord you learn is like learning 12 new chords since any of the 12 notes of the chromatic scale can be the root note of any type of chord.

2.) The particular family *(Major, minor or Dominant)* each new chord formation belongs to. Force yourself to hear each new chord in those terms.

A command over lots of chords is essential to great playing. A few good **chord solos** (such as the tune *"Lenny"* by Stevie Ray Vaughn) are a welcome addition to any guitarist's repertoire. Playing a series of short funky chords makes a nice change of pace from boring old cliché rock riffs (i.e. tunes like *"Under the Bridge"* by the Red Hot Chili Peppers or *"Come On- part II"* by Jimi Hendrix).

One mark of a good guitarist is the ability to play beautiful instrumental solos . Joe Pass and Wes Montgomery were masters of a wonderful style called **chord melody**. This means that the chords *and* the melody are played at the same time on one guitar. Try it!

Think of a chord vocabulary the way a painter views his palette -selecting just the right color from many for the perfect effect. A good way to work on your chords is to have a large repertoire of songs in a variety of styles. Below, I've suggested a few unusual & interesting tunes which should be studied with *very accurate* sheet music, a recording or a professional music teacher.

Rock	Blues	Jazz	Other
All Right Now	Stormy Monday	"A Train"	Minuet in G
Sultans Of Swing	Help Me	Satin Doll	El Paso
Oye Como Va	All Your Lovin'	Caravan	Malaguena
Black Magic Women	Killin Floor	All Of Me	Romance
Wind Cries Mary	Red House	Just Friends	Folsom Prison
Lay Lady Lay	Bring It On Home	Bill Bailey	Vincent
50 Ways to Leave Lover	St. Louis Blues	Take 5	Havah Nagilah
Lean On Me	St. James Infirmary	In The Mood	Pink Panther
Stray Cat Strut	Hucklebuck	Jersey Bounce	Hey Gd Lookin'
Oh! Darlin	Thrill is gone	Ipenama	Cheatin Heart
Heatwave	Boom Boom Boom	Georgia	Aloha Oe
Yesterday	Boogie Chillin	Over Rainbow	America
When I'm 64	Dust My Broom	Bye Bye Blackbird	
L.A. Women		Ain't Misbehavin'	

Learning some songs from this reference will help you to avoid ruts and give you exposure to some excellent ideas. To become a "complete" guitarist, study chord progressions from all the styles of music which speak to you. The great Duke Ellington once said, "There's only two types of music- good & bad."

Key: Reading Chord Graphs

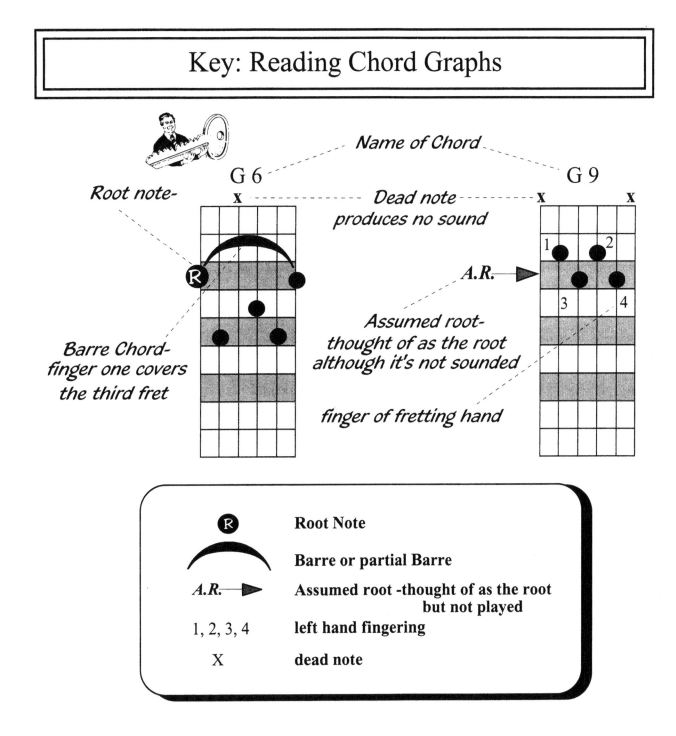

Name of Chord

G 6

G 9

Root note-

X

Dead note
produces no sound

X   X

A.R.→

Assumed root-
thought of as the root
although it's not sounded

Barre Chord-
finger one covers
the third fret

finger of fretting hand

®	Root Note
⌒	Barre or partial Barre
A.R.→	Assumed root -thought of as the root but not played
1, 2, 3, 4	left hand fingering
X	dead note

A concept central to understanding the Guitar:

Any type of movable chord can have any one of twelve possible root notes. They are:

A *A#/Bb* **B** **C** *C#/Db* **D** *D#/Bb* **E** **F** *F#/Gb* **G** *G#/Ab* **A**

....the notes of the chromatic scale. Therefore, the first chord diagram above, "G *6*", could just as easily be named *and played as "A 6", "Bb 6", "B 6", "C 6","C# 6", "D 6"*, and so on. Each one of these chords would be diagrammed exactly the same way, differing only in their location on the neck. Most books print each and every one of these movable chords 12 separate times. This is really not necessary if you understand the simple principle of movable chords.

ROOT 6 MOVABLE CHORDS: G *MAJOR FAMILY*

G 5
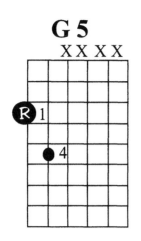

G 6
G 6
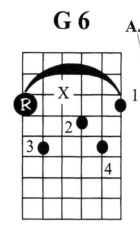
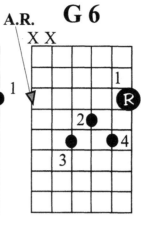

G Ma 7
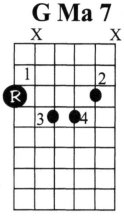

G Ma 7
G Ma 7
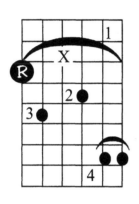
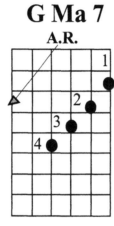

G add 9
G add 9
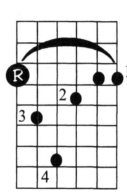
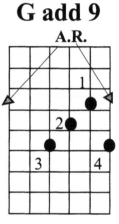

G add 9
G 6/9
G 6/9
G Ma 13
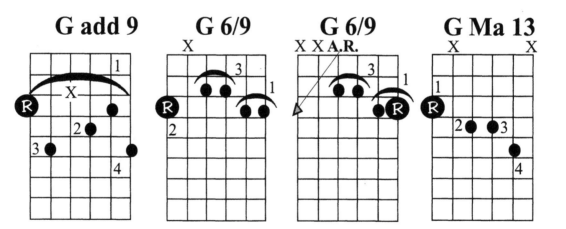

🎸 These Root 6 Major type chords are playable *anywhere* on the neck.

🎸 All Major chords produce the same overall sound quality.

C 5
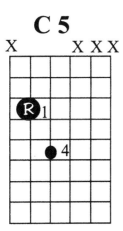

C 6
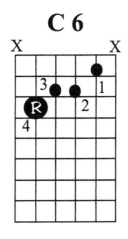

C 6
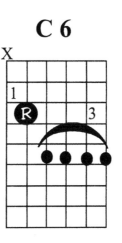

C Ma 7
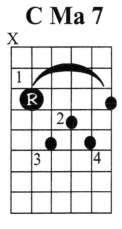

C Ma 9
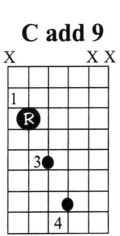

C add 9

C add 9
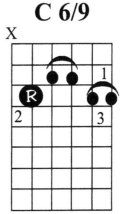

C 6/9

🎸 These Root 5 Major type chords are playable *anywhere* on the neck.

🎸 Any C Major type chord can substitute for any other C Major type chord .

Move and play these chords all over the neck. Practice naming the resulting root notes.

Think of every chord on page 54 as a **ROOT 6 CHORD.** Played and named in relation to its root note: **"G",** string 6, fret III.

Think of every chord this page as a **ROOT 5 CHORD.** Played and named in relation to its root note: **"C",** string 5, fret III.

ROOT 6 MOVABLE CHORDS: G *MINOR FAMILY*

G mi 6   G mi 7   G mi 7   G mi 7

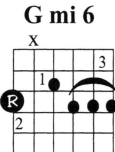
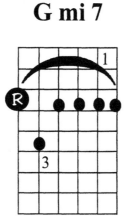
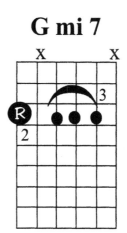
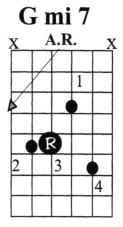

G mi 9   G mi 9   G mi 7 sus   G mi 11

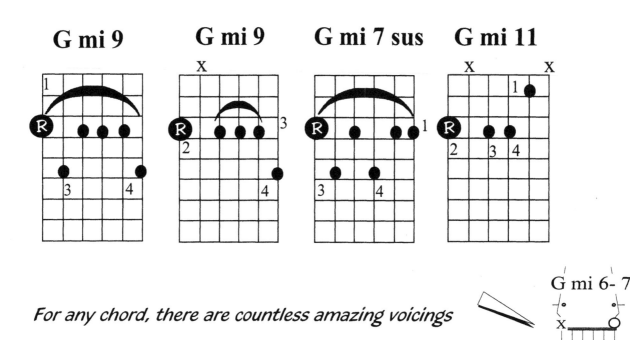

For any chord, there are countless amazing voicings

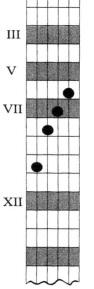

G mi 6- 7

🎸 These Root 6 minor type chords are playable *anywhere* on the neck.

🎸 All G minor chords produce the overall sound and can substitute for each other.

🎸 G mi 7 has the same basic shape as a A mi 7, Bb mi 7, B mi 7, C mi 7, and so on.

ROOT 5 MOVABLE CHORDS: C *MINOR FAMILY*

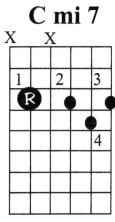

C mi 7

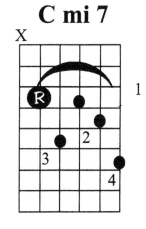

C mi 7

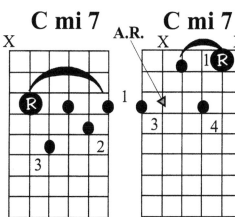

C mi 7   C mi 7

C mi 7

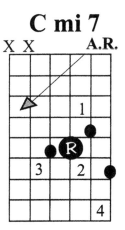

C mi 7   C mi 9   C mi 7 sus   C mi 7 sus

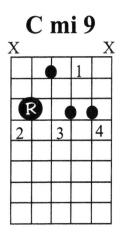

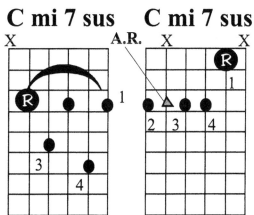

Chord shapes make excellent lead guitar lines.

..IF THE ONLY THING YOU HAVE IS A HAMMER, EVERYTHING LOOKS LIKE A NAIL.

C mi 9

ROOT 6 MOVABLE CHORDS: G *DOMINANT 7 FAMILY*

G 7 **G 7** **G 7(b5)** **G 7(#5)**

G 9 **G 7(b9)** **G 7(#9)** **G 13**

G 7 sus **G 9(#5)** **G 13** **G 7(#5 b9)**

These chords are particularly useful in lead blues guitar.

For a complete discussion of the theory of Dominant 11th, Dominant 7th sus, minor 11th, and minor 7th sus, see page 84 of this book.

C 7
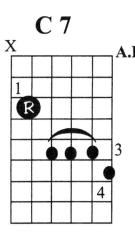

C 7
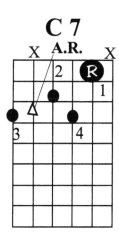

C 7
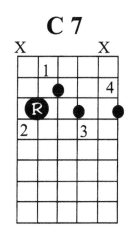

C 7
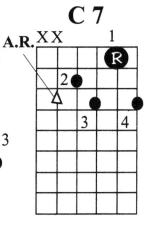

C 7(b5)
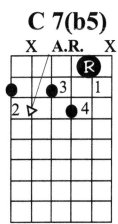

C 9
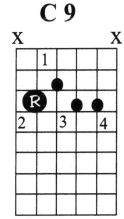

C 9
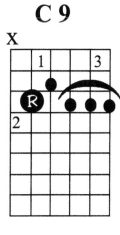

C 7(b9)
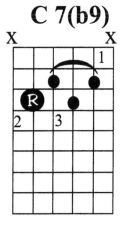

C 7 sus
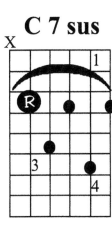

C 7 sus
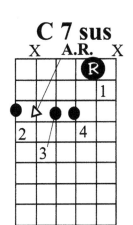

C 7(#9)
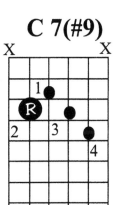

C 13
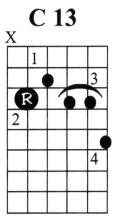

All serious musicians practice everything they learn in all 12 keys. Use the circle of fifths and the chromatic scale as guides for practicing.

Line Clichés

Line Clichés are chord sequences in which one note changes while the other notes in the chord stay the same. These rich and beautiful sounds are worthy of careful study. Line Clichés are quite difficult to hear and play when they have not first been studied.

This will conclude our introduction to the Root six and Root five system of guitar playing. Several new individual chord forms are presented as part of the line clichés. These new chords are also useful in their own right.

minor, minor-Major 7th, minor 7th, minor 6th -*Root 6*

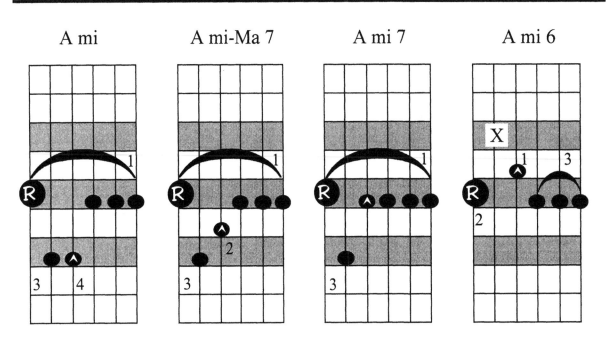

minor, minor-Major 7th, minor 7th, minor 6th -*Root 5*

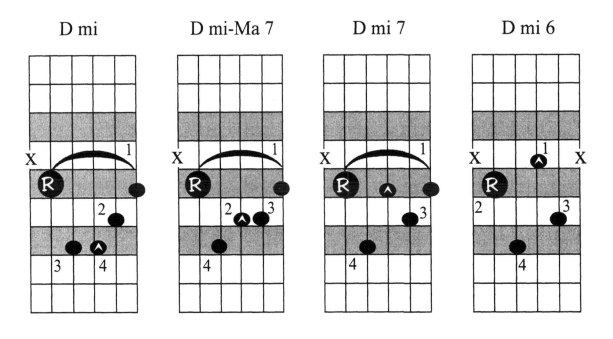

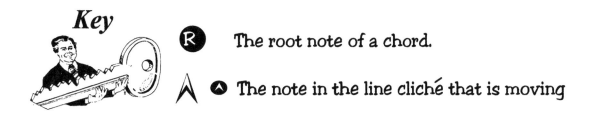
minor, minor-Major 7th, minor 7th, minor 6th -*Root 5 (or Root 2)*

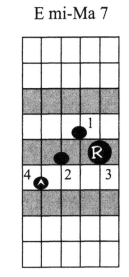

minor, minor-Major 7th, minor 7th, minor 6th,-*Root 4*

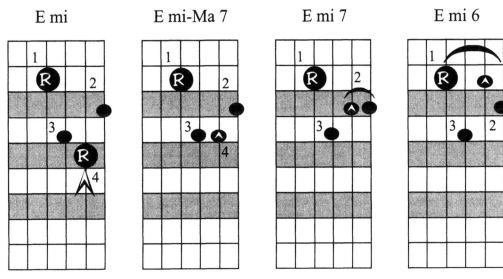

Common symbols for the minor line cliché:

Ami, Ami△, A mi6, A mi7,
A -, A -(Ma 7), A -6, A -7,

minor, minor (#5), minor 6th -*Root 6*

| A mi | A mi (#5) | A mi 6 | A mi (#5) |

minor, minor (#5), minor 6th -*Root 5*

| D mi | D mi (#5) | D mi 6 | D mi (#5) |

When a song has one static chord for several measures, line clichés are used to spice things up. The minor line clichés are a real favorite among songwriters. *Stairway to Heaven, Time in a Bottle, Sunny, My Funny Valentine* and the *007 Theme* are examples of famous tunes which employ line clichés.

As an arranger or writer *(read: "guitarist in original rock band")*, line clichés will give your work a professional, sophisticated sound. The compositional device of line clichés alleviates the **"Garage band hanging on one chord"** type of effect.

These chords are also valuable for creating interesting guitar solos based on one chord. Most guitarists employ chord shapes and "broken" chords as part of their improvisational vocabulary. Using your fingers to "trace out" the shapes of a line cliché will add *"zip"* to your lead playing.

Major, Augmented, 6th, Dominant 7th -***Root 4***

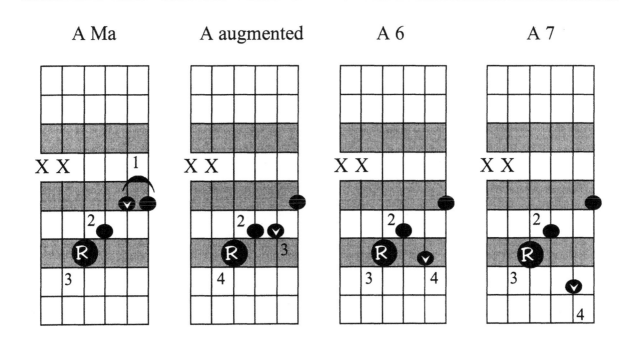

Major, Augmented, 6th, Dominant 7th,-***Root 5***

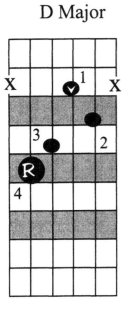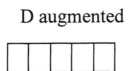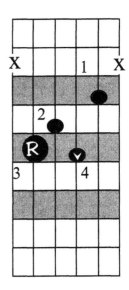

Major, Major 7th, 6th, Dominant 7th -*Root 6*

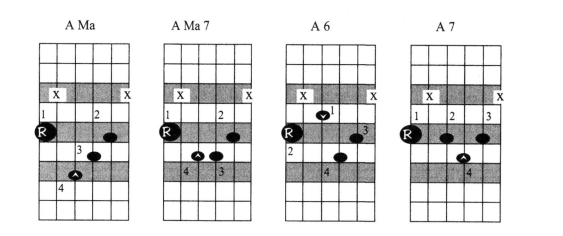

Major, Augmented, 6th, Dominant 7th -*Root 5*

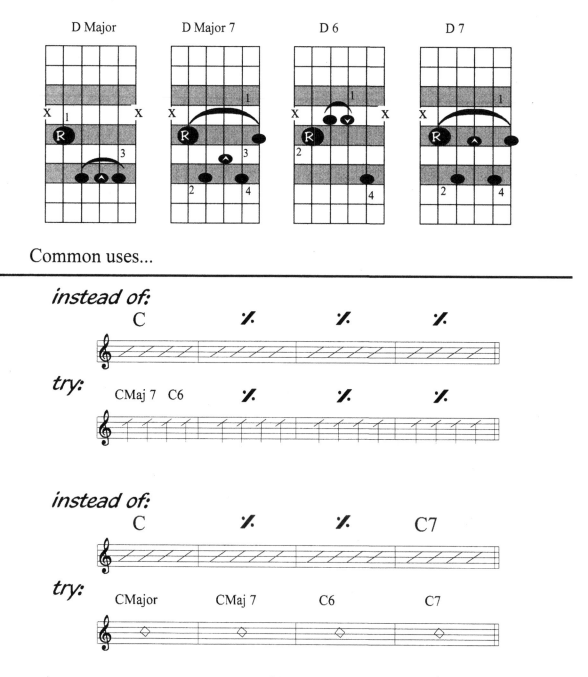

Common uses...

instead of:

try:

instead of:

try:

Major, Major 7th, 6th, Dominant 7th -*Root 5*

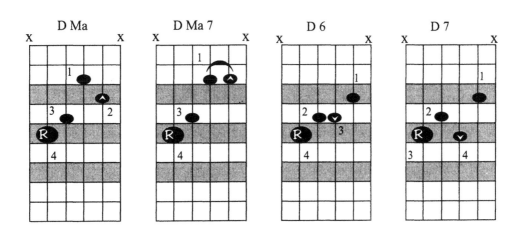

Major, Augmented, 6th, Dominant 7th -*Root 4*

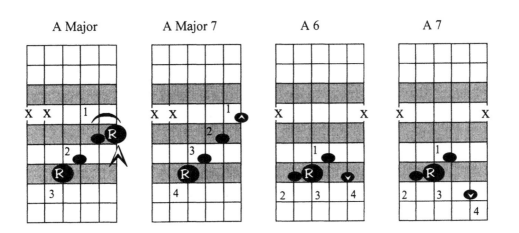

Major, Augmented, 6th, Dominant 7th -*Root 5 (or Root 3)*

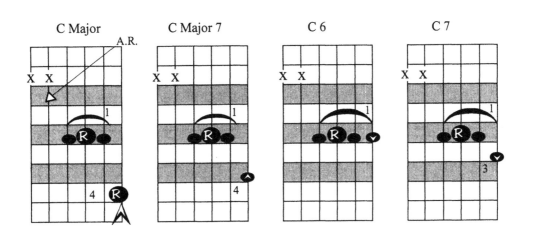

THERE ARE TWO CLEFS:

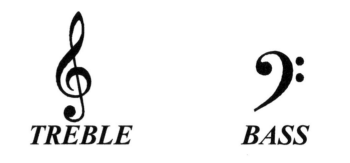

To understand music theory, all guitarists must be acquainted with the traditional **Grand Staff** and how to name the notes on it. Study and refer to the charts below.

TREBLE

For the higher notes

BASS

For the lower notes

The Clefs are each placed on their own *Staff*.

Notes are placed on the various lines and spaces on the staff to indicate different pitches.

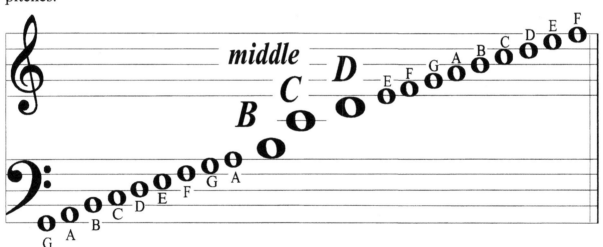

Notes too high or low to be on the staff are placed on *Ledger Lines.*

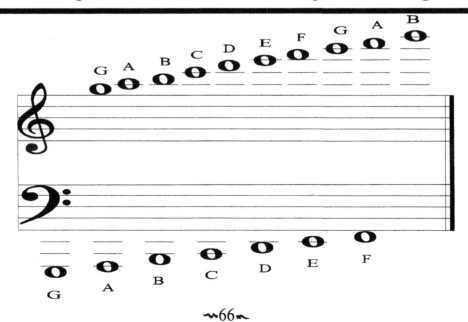

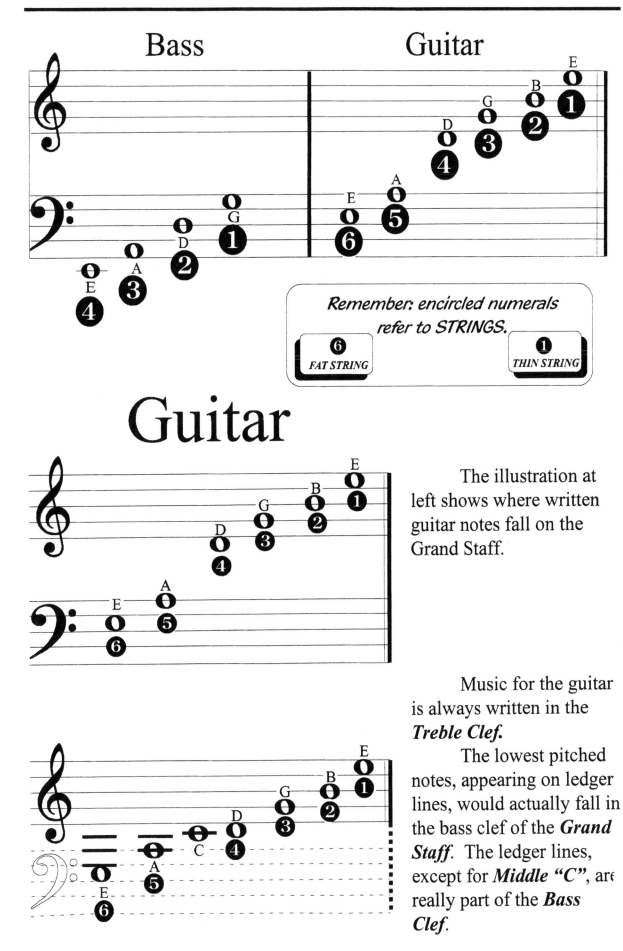

Guitar

The illustration at left shows where written guitar notes fall on the Grand Staff.

Music for the guitar is always written in the **Treble Clef.**

The lowest pitched notes, appearing on ledger lines, would actually fall in the bass clef of the **Grand Staff**. The ledger lines, except for **Middle "C"**, are really part of the **Bass Clef**.

The complete notes of the Guitar.

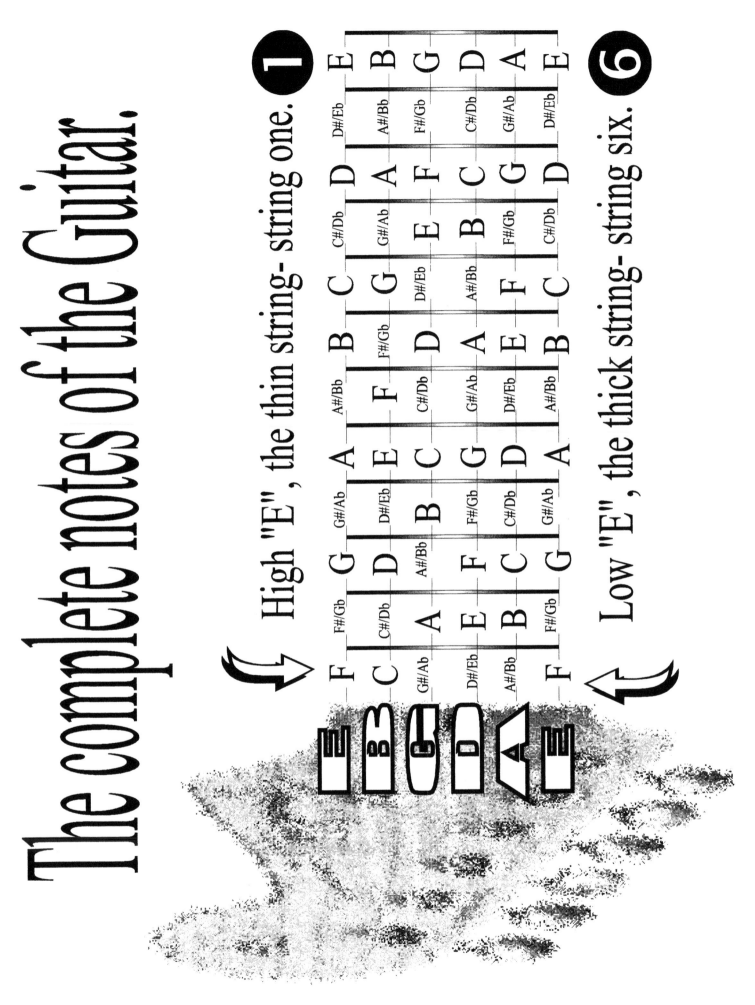

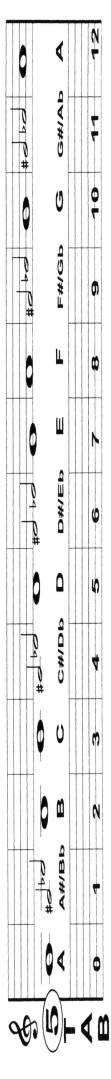
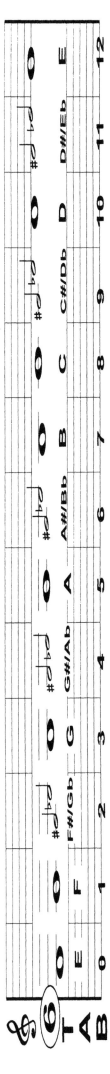

REVIEW

Chromatic Scale: All 12 musical notes played or written in adjacent order.

A *A#/Bb* B C *C#/Db* D *D#/Eb* E F *F#Gb* G *G#/Ab* A

Major Scale Formula: The exact and specific order of intervals separating the notes of any Major scale is:

Do *whole* **Re** *whole* **Mi** *1/2* **Fa** *whole* **Sol** *whole* **La** *whole* **Ti** *1/2* **Do**

C Major, For Example:

C	D	E	F	G	A	B	C
W	W	½	W	W	W	½	

THE TWELVE KEYS

There are 12 notes in the chromatic scale. Any one of the notes 12 can be the root note of its own Major scale. Each new Major scale is the center of its own little musical world or *Key*. Each Major scale contains a unique combination of notes.

Sharp Keys: Major Scales that need to use sharped notes to follow the scale formula and create the sound of a Major scale:

G	A	B	C	D	E	F#	G	***G Major; 1 Sharp***
D	E	F#	G	A	B	C#	D	***D Major; 2 Sharps***
A	B	C#	D	E	F#	G#	A	***A Major; 3 Sharps***
E	F#	G#	A	B	C#	D#	E	***E Major; 4 Sharps***
B	C#	D#	E	F#	G#	A#	B	***B Major; 5 Sharps***
F#	G#	A#	B	C#	D#	E#	F#	***F# Major; 6 Sharps***

Flat Keys: Major Scales that need to use flatted notes to follow the scale formula and create the sound of a Major scale:

F	G	A	B♭	C	D	E	F	***F Major; 1 Flat***
B♭	C	D	E	F	G	A	B♭	***B♭ Major; 2 Flats***
E♭	F	G	A	B♭	C	D	E♭	***E♭ Major; 3 Flats***
A♭	B♭	C	D	E♭	F	G	A♭	***A♭ Major; 4 Flats***
D♭	E♭	F	G♭	A♭	B♭	C	D♭	***D♭ Major; 5 Flats***
G♭	A♭	B♭	C♭	D♭	E♭	F	G♭	***G♭ Major; 6 Flats***

THE KEY SIGNATURES

The musical staffs below illustrate key signatures. Each key has a unique **Key signature** which relates directly to the number of flats or sharps its Major scale contains. To illustrate, The key of **'G'** has one sharped note: **'F'**. The **Key Signature** for this key has a sharp symbol placed on the line that an F note might occupy. This means that **any and all** the F notes in the music following this particular **Key Signature** are to be played as **F sharps**. A **Key Signature** is always placed directly after the clef (𝄞).

Experienced musicians instantly recognize any *Key Signature*.

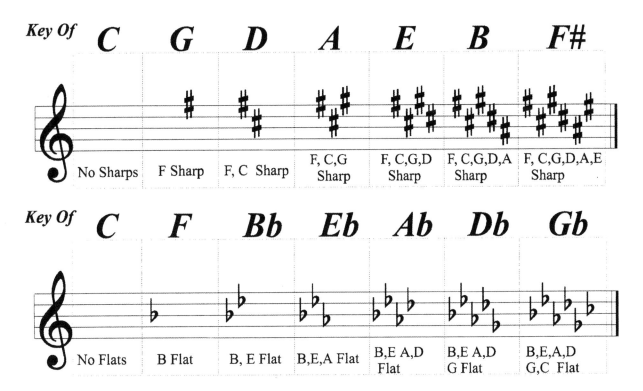

~71~

Theoretical Basis of Chords

Chords are analyzed in two ways: by *Formula* and by *Spelling*.

CHORD FORMULAS

All chords of a particular quality possess the same *formula.* Any chord formula is based on the Major scale. A **C Major** chord for example, contains only three notes: **C, E & G.**

When we examine a C Major scale its evident that the notes: **C, E & G** are the **first, third & fifth** notes of the scale.

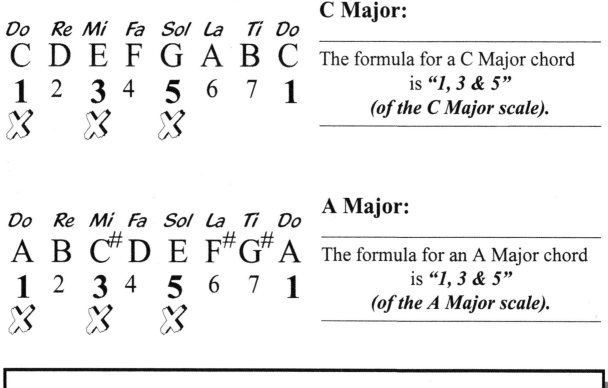

C Major:

The formula for a C Major chord is *"1, 3 & 5"* *(of the C Major scale).*

A Major:

The formula for an A Major chord is *"1, 3 & 5"* *(of the A Major scale).*

> *Any Major type chord has the chord formula 1, 3 & 5. This means that all major chords are comprised of the first, third and fifth notes of their respective Major scales.*

CHORD SPELLINGS

A chord's spelling is the exact letter names of the individual notes that make up the chord. Unlike chord formulas, chord spellings are unique for every chord. The spelling of a chord belongs to that chord only.

In the examples above, the A Major chord *(spelled A, C# & E)* and the C Major chord *(spelled C, E & G)* each have the same **formula**: 1, 3 & 5 of their respective Major scales.

THE 3 BASIC CHORD TYPES IN THE KEYS OF 'A' & 'C'.

Examine the three basic chord types with root notes of either **C** or **A**. Notice how they relate to their respective Major scales. *(illustrated on page 72* ↻)

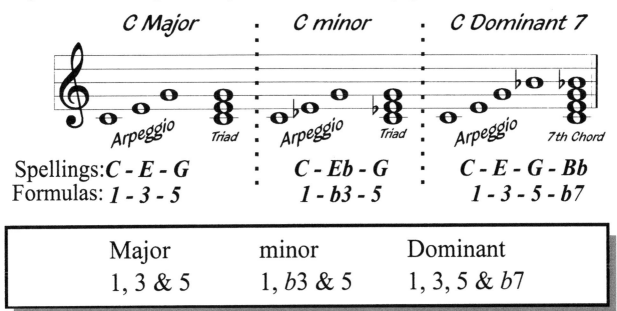

Spellings: *C - E - G* : *C - Eb - G* : *C - E - G - Bb*
Formulas: *1 - 3 - 5* : *1 - b3 - 5* : *1 - 3 - 5 - b7*

Major	minor	Dominant
1, 3 & 5	1, *b*3 & 5	1, 3, 5 & *b*7

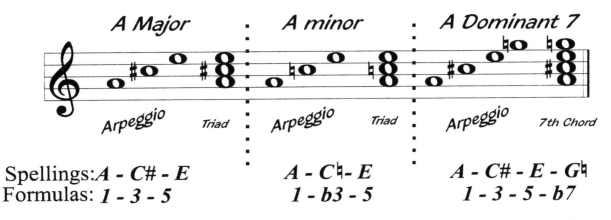

Spellings: *A - C# - E* : *A - C♮- E* : *A - C# - E - G♮*
Formulas: *1 - 3 - 5* : *1 - b3 - 5* : *1 - 3 - 5 - b7*

The A Major scale contains 3 sharps *(A, B, C#, D, E, F#, G#, A)*. The naturally occurring third note of the A Major scale is *C#*. A plain old *'C'* or *'C natural'* (C ♮), is the *flatted third* note of the A Major scale *(which normally has C# as its third member)*.

The naturally occurring seventh note of the A Major scale is *'G#'*. A plain old *'G natural'* (G ♮) is the *flatted seventh* note of the A Major scale *(which normally has G# as its seventh member)*.

DEFINITIONS

Arpeggio- The individual notes of a chord played or written in order.

Triad- Chords containing three notes.

7th chords- A 4 note chord. A seventh chord has a basic triad plus the natural or flatted seventh degree of the Major scale.

Diminished & Augmented chords.

Diminished and augmented triads are each in their own special categories. At first, these chords sound somewhat unusual. Augmented 7th chords are a favorite for producing tension. The diminished 7th voicings make excellent "passing" chords.

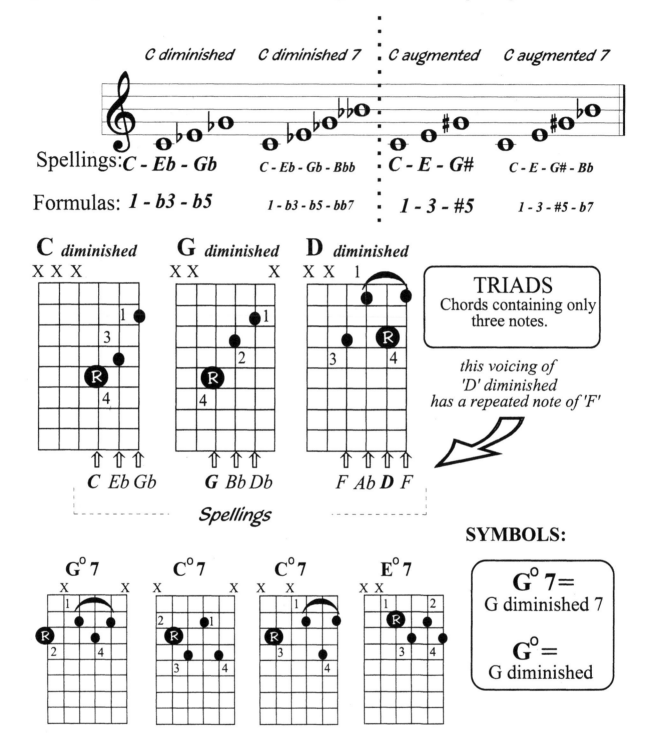

Spellings: C - Eb - Gb   C - Eb - Gb - Bbb   C - E - G#   C - E - G# - Bb

Formulas: 1 - b3 - b5   1 - b3 - b5 - bb7   1 - 3 - #5   1 - 3 - #5 - b7

C diminished   **G** diminished   **D** diminished

C Eb Gb   G Bb Db   F Ab **D** F

Spellings

TRIADS
Chords containing only three notes.

this voicing of 'D' diminished has a repeated note of 'F'

SYMBOLS:

G°7   C°7   C°7   E°7

G° 7 =
G diminished 7

G° =
G diminished

Diminished triads can sound thin and be awkward to play. Therefore, in playing situations that call for a 'diminished chord', most guitarists use one of the 'diminished 7' chords illustrated above as a substitute.

Diminished 7 chords have 2 very useful and unusual qualities:

1.)Any note in any diminished 7 chord can be called the root note of the chord.
   Diminished 7 chords have 4 possible roots and therefore 4 possible names.
Diminished triads **do not** have this quality.

> # *C diminished 7 is spelled C - Eb - Gb - Bbb*
> ## *Therefore a C°7 chord = an Eb°7chord*
> ## *= an Gb°7chord = an A°7chord*
>
> $$B^{\flat\flat} = A^{\natural}$$

2.)Any diminished 7 chord repeats itself every 3 frets.
These repeated chords, called inversions, perform exactly the function as each other and
can substitute for each other. Diminished *triads* **do not** have this quality.

Inversions of *C diminished*	Inversions of *C diminished*	Inversions of *C diminished*	Inversions of *G diminished*

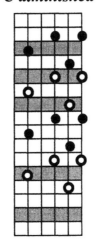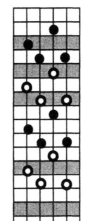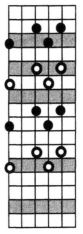

Augmented Chords

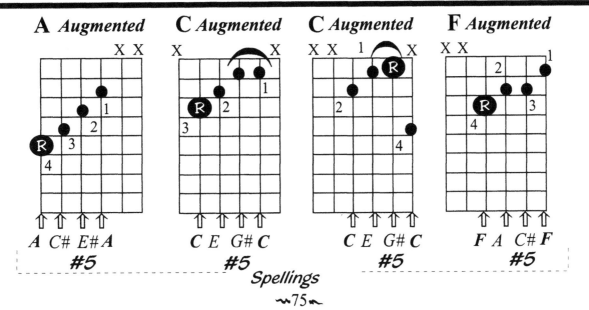

A *Augmented*	**C** *Augmented*	**C** *Augmented*	**F** *Augmented*
A C# E# A	C E G# C	C E G# C	F A C# F
#5	#5	#5	#5

Spellings

Augmented Chords have 2 very useful and unusual qualities:

1.)Any note in the chord can be called the root of the chord.
Augmented chords have 3 possible roots and therefore 3 possible names. Augmented 7 **do not** have this quality.

C augmented is spelled C - E - G#

Therefore a C aug chord = an E aug chord
= a G# aug chord

2.)Any augmented chord repeats itself every 4 frets.
These inversions perform exactly the function as each other and can substitute for each other. Augmented *7th's* **do not** have this quality.

Inversions of *C augmented*	Inversions of *F augmented*	Inversions of *A augmented*	Inversions of *E augmented*	

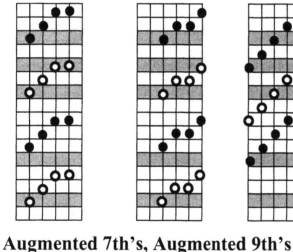

C Augmented =

C Aug. *or* C+

Augmented 7th's, Augmented 9th's

G Augmented 7:
➤ *G 7 +*
➤ *G7 (#5)*
➤ *G 7 Aug.*
-all 3 symbols mean the same thing.

G 7 +   G 9 +   C 7 +   C 9 +

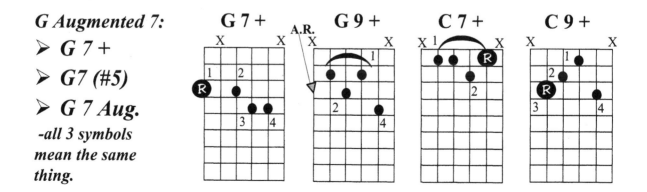

The distance between two notes is called an **interval.** When identifying a musical interval it is always assumed that the lowest pitched note *(of the two notes in the interval)* is the root note or **"DO"** of a Major scale.

DIATONIC INTERVALS

These are intervals based entirely on a Major scale. The Diatonic intervals for the key of 'C' are illustrated below.

Do	Re	Mi	Fa	Sol	La	Ti	Do
C	D	E	F	G	A	B	C
1	2	3	4	5	6	7	1
							(8th)

'D' is the **second** note of a **C Major Scale.** It's said that *"D is the 2nd of C Major."*
The distance between the note 'C' and the note 'D' is a Major 2nd.

'E' is the **third** note of a **C Major Scale.** It's said that *"E is the 3rd of C Major."*
The distance between the note 'C' and the note 'E' is a Major 3rd.

'F' is the **fourth** note of a **C Major Scale.** It's said that *"F is the 4th of C Major."*
The distance between the note 'C' and the note 'F' is a Perfect 4th.

'G' is the **fifth** note of a **C Major Scale.** It's said that *"G is the 5th of C Major."*
The distance between the note 'C' and the note 'G' is a Perfect 5th.

'A' is the **sixth** note of a **C Major Scale.** It's said that *"A is the 6th of C Major."*
The distance between the note 'C' and the note 'A' is a Major 6th.

'B' is the **seventh** note of a **C Major Scale.** It's said that *"B is the 7th of C Major."*
The distance between the note 'C' and the note 'B' is a Major 7th.

'C' is the **octave** *(the first but also the eighth note)* of a **C Major Scale.**
The distance between the two 'C' notes is a Perfect Octave.

COMPOUND INTERVALS

Intervals based on a Major Scale but separated by a distance of more than one octave are called *compound intervals*. Below are two octaves of the C major scale.

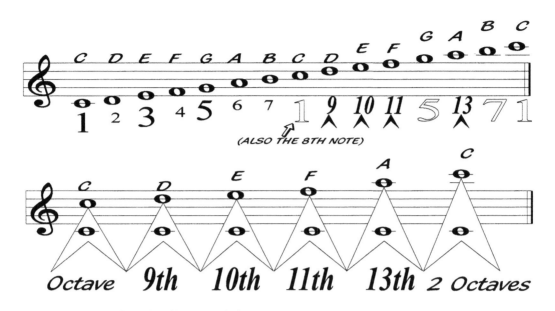

NON-DIATONIC INTERVALS

These are any two notes in the chromatic scale, which can be given an intervallic name. Below are all possible non-diatonic intervals with 'C' as the root.

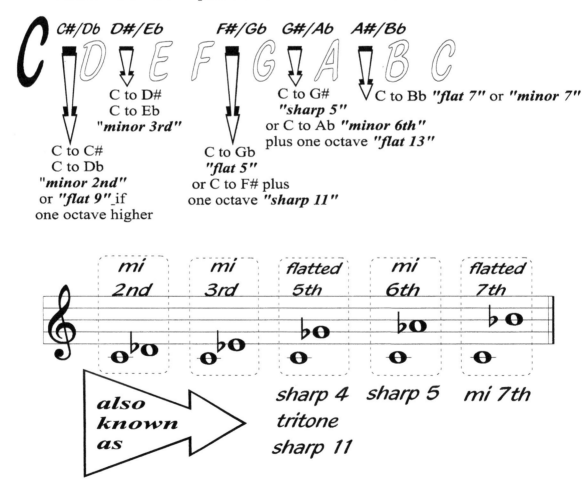

Advanced Chord Formulas and Spellings

All chord types all have colorful brothers and sisters as members of their families. These chords, called *extended harmonies*, are named in terms of the scale tones they contain in addition to a basic chord. Chords names like : **C Major 7, C minor 9** or **C 13** for example.

A chord named **C Major 7** would contain the three notes of a basic **C Major** chord *(called a Triad)* and the 7th degree *(called a Tension)* of the C major scale .

C MAJOR 7
Formula: 1 3 5 7 *Spelling:* C E G B

Most Common Major Chords

Name	Formula	Spelling
C MAJOR	1 3 5	C E G
C 6	1 3 5 6	C E G A
C MAJOR 7	1 3 5 7	C E G B
C add 9	1 3 5 9	C E G D
C MAJOR 9	1 3 5 7 9	C E G B D
C 6/9	1 3 5 6 9	C E G D A
C MAJOR 13	1 3 5 7 9 13	C E G B D A
C MAJOR 7(#11)	1 3 5 7 #11	C E G B F#

Chord Name	Prevalant Symbols
C Major	C
C Major 7	C Ma 7, C 7, C△
C Major 9	C Ma 9, C△9
C 6/9	C 6/9
C Major 13	C△13

Most Common minor Chords

Name	Formula	Spelling
C minor	1 b3 5	C Eb G
C minor 6	1 b3 5 6	C Eb G A
C minor 7	1 b3 5 b7	C Eb G Bb
C minor 7(SUS 4)	1 4 5 b7	C F G Bb
C minor 9	1 b3 5 b7 9	C Eb G Bb D
C minor 11	1 b3 5 b7 11	C Eb G Bb D F

NOTE; For playing purposes Cmi 11 & Cmi 7sus can be used interchangeably -freely substituted for one another.

Chord Name	Prevalant Symbols
C minor	C-, C m, C mi
C minor 7	C mi 7, C- 7,
C minor 9	C mi 9, C- 9
C minor 11	C mi 11, C- 11

Most Common Triads

Name	Formula	Spelling
C MAJOR	1 3 5	C E G
C minor	1 b3 5	C Eb G A
C Augmented	1 3 #5	C E G#
C Diminished	1 b3 b5	C Eb Gb

Chord Name	Prevalant Symbols
C augmented	C+, C aug.
C diminished	C dim, C°

Most Common Dominant Chords

Name	Formula	Spelling
C 7	1 3 5 *b*7	C E G Bb
C 9	1 3 5 *b*7 9	C E G Bb D
C 11	1 3 5 *b*7 9 11	C E G Bb D F
C 13	1 3 5 *b*7 9 13	C E G Bb D A
C 7sus	1 4 5 *b*7	C F G Bb
C *diminished* 7	1 *b*3 *b*5 *bb*7	C Eb Gb Bbb *(B double flat a.k.a A natural)*
C *augmented* 7	1 3 #5 *b*7	C E G# Bb *(C augmented 7 a.k.a C7 #5)*
C 7(b5)	1 3 *b*5 *b*7	C E Gb Bb

NOTE; For playing purposes, chord forms for C 11 & C 7sus are generally thought of as the same thing.

Chord Name	Prevalant Symbols
C Dominant 7	C 7
C Dominant 9	C 9
C Dominant 11	C 11
C Dominant 13	C 13
C Augmented 7	C 7 (#5), C7+
C Dominant 7(b5)	C 7 (b5)
C Diminished 7	C°7
C7 Suspended	C 7 sus

Slash Chords

"Slash chords" are chords which indicate the use of a specific bass note along with a particular chord - *"G over A"* for example.

Basic G Major chord
(Spelled G - B - D) ⤢ G/A ⬉ *Specific bass note, "A" to be played as the lowest pitched note along with the basic G chord*

Below are some common slash chords in the keys of C & G. All G forms will be based on a ***Root six*** G Major. All C forms will be based on a ***Root five*** C Major so that these 'new' forms can be easily transposed:

3rd in Bass	5th in Bass	9th in Bass
C/E	C/G	C/D
G/B	G/D	G/A

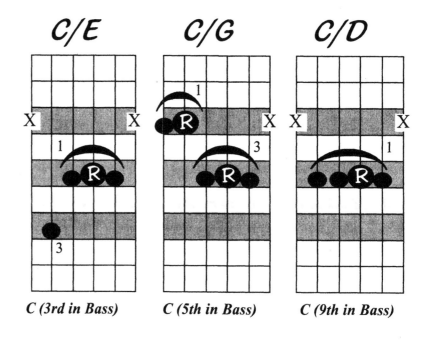

Root 5 C Major   C/E   C/G   C/D

C (3rd in Bass)   C (5th in Bass)   C (9th in Bass)

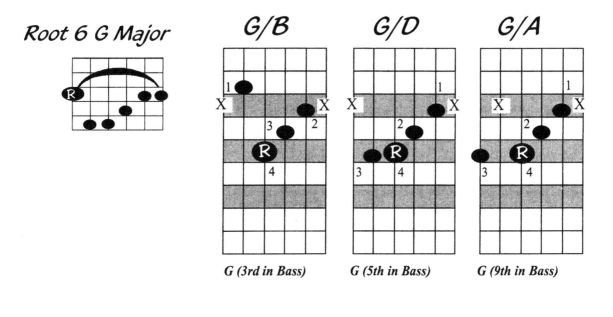

Root 6 G Major

G/B — G (3rd in Bass)

G/D — G (5th in Bass)

G/A — G (9th in Bass)

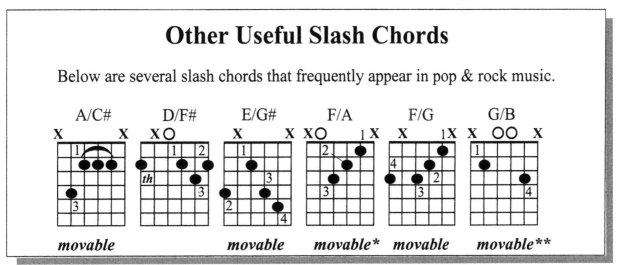

Other Useful Slash Chords

Below are several slash chords that frequently appear in pop & rock music.

A/C# — _movable_

D/F# — _movable_

E/G# — _movable*_

F/A — _movable_

F/G — _movable**_

G/B

Slash chords are useful in playing bass lines with chord progressions or providing motion and interest on a prolonged chord.

A wonderful compositional device, slash chords are common in the music of **Steely Dan, Neil Young, The Beatles, Paul Simon** and jazz greats **Pat Metheny** and **Mick Goodrick.**

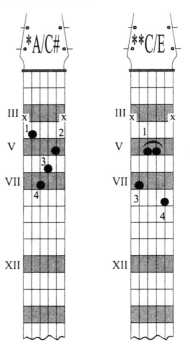

*A/C#

**C/E

Key: Suspended chords & 11th chords.

The **dominant 11th, suspended 7th, minor 11th** and **minor 7th suspended** chords can be somewhat tricky. The shapes associated with these beautiful chord voicings are often useful in a variety of situations. In the realm of **dominant 11th, sus. 7th, minor 11th** and **minor 7th sus.** chords, one form *("shape")* can have several different names and perform a variety of functions.

Dominant 7 sus & mi 7 sus:

A *suspended chord* is one in which the third, be it a **Major third** or a **minor third**, is replaced by a **fourth**.

C 7 sus is spelled		C F G Bb
C mi 7 sus is spelled		C F G Bb

> *These two chords have the exact same spelling. Therefore, a chord shape known C 7 sus can function as C-7sus and vice versa. In other words, they share fingerings.*

Dominant 11th & mi 11th:

A *eleventh chord* is one in which the 11th note of the scale (*4th plus an octave*) is added to a **Dominant chord** or a **minor chord**. In this case, the third of the chord is left in its original place.

C 11 is spelled		C *E* G Bb F
C mi 11 is spelled		C *Eb* G Bb F

> *A difference in spellings -meaning these two chords <u>can not</u> always share fingerings.*

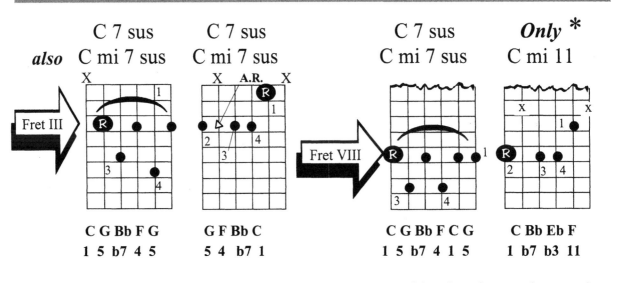

also	C 7 sus	C 7 sus	C 7 sus	*Only* *
	C mi 7 sus	C mi 7 sus	C mi 7 sus	C mi 11

Fret III

Fret VIII

C G Bb F G	**G F Bb C**	**C G Bb F C G**	**C Bb Eb F**
1 5 b7 4 5	**5 4 b7 1**	**1 5 b7 4 1 5**	**1 b7 b3 11**

~84~   ***** Because this chord contains a minor third, DO NOT think of it as C 7 sus or C 11.

COMMON TONES

Common tones are notes shared by two or more chords. In the case of *C 7 sus,* *C mi 7 sus, C 11 & Cmi 11* the common tones are the notes **C, F, G, & Bb.** Any of the first three chords on page 84 could *theoretically* function as either *C 7 sus, C mi 7 sus, C 11 or Cmi 11.* Quite often, sheet music and guitar magazines will use either of these three chord formations in songs calling for *C 7 sus, C mi 7 sus, C 11 or Cmi 11.* This "common tones only" approach can be a real lifesaver for getting the job done but is somewhat of an oversimplification.

Any chord containing a **minor third** should not be thought of as a *dominant 7 sus* chord. Any chord containing a **MAJOR third** should not be thought of as a *minor 7 sus* chord. Below is an examination of the same 4 chords illustrated on page 84 except with a "G" root note.

Dominant 7 sus & mi 7 sus:

G 7 sus is spelled	G C D F
G mi 7 sus is spelled	G C D F

> *The spellings are the same . Therefore, a chord shape known G 7 sus can function as Gmi7sus and vice versa.*

Dominant 11th & mi 11th:

G 11 is spelled	G **B** D F C
G mi 11 is spelled	G **Bb** D F C

> *A difference in the spellings -these two chords can not always share fingerings.*

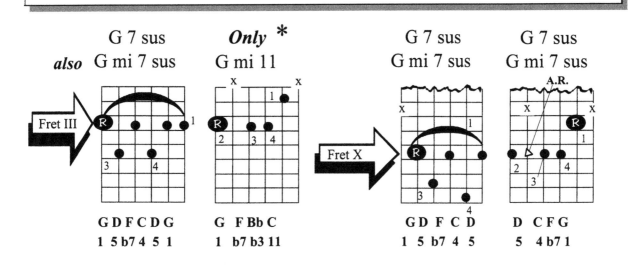

*Because this chord contains a minor third, DO NOT think of as G 7 sus or G 11.

FIVE POSITION THINKING

The cornerstone of advanced and pro guitar playing is undoubtedly playing and thinking in five logical, interconnected positions. This means that for every chord on the guitar there are five successive chord shapes or "grips". These 5 shapes form a chord pattern which is 6 strings wide and 12 frets long. Each of the twelve major chords has a 12 fret *"super pattern"*.

A **C Major** chord, for example:

C	D	E	F	G	A	B	C
1st	2nd	*3rd*	4th	*5th*	6th	7th	1st
(do	re	mi	fa	sol	la	ti	do)

	Spelling :	C	E	G
	Formula :	1	3	5

Any time the three notes **C, E, & G** are played together a C Major chord sound is the result. If we now highlight every **C, E, & G** on a guitar neck the need for a system of position playing is evident. Just think of all the possible ways to play some type of C Major chord. Maybe even one that is yours alone.

On the following pages, you'll find the **C Major** and **G Major** chords diagrammed in terms of all the available chord tones within the first 12 frets of a guitar. *Five basic chord shapes* -with suggested fingerings have been extracted from the super patterns. This system of 5 position thinking is the cornerstone of modern playing.

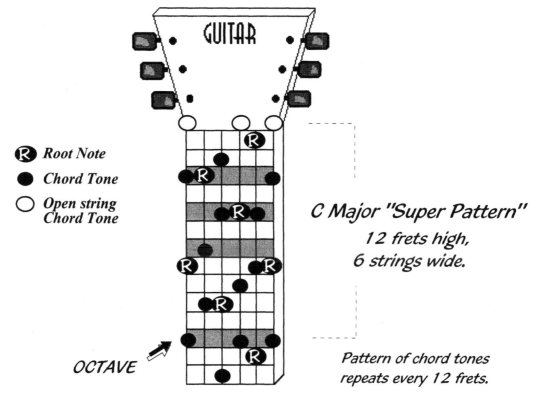

Ⓡ *Root Note*

● *Chord Tone*

○ *Open string Chord Tone*

C Major "Super Pattern"
12 frets high,
6 strings wide.

OCTAVE

Pattern of chord tones repeats every 12 frets.

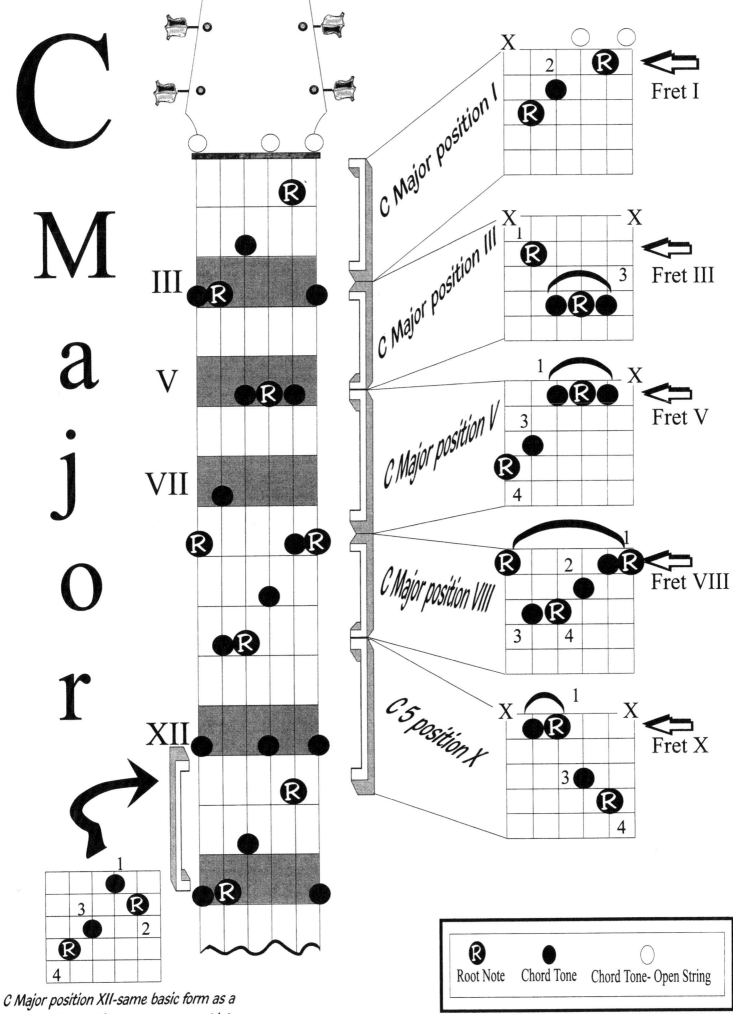

C Major

C Major position I — Fret I

C Major position III — Fret III

C Major position V — Fret V

C Major position VIII — Fret VIII

C 5 position X — Fret X

III
V
VII
XII

Root Note — Chord Tone — Chord Tone- Open String

C Major position XII-same basic form as a
plain old 'open C' except one octave higher.

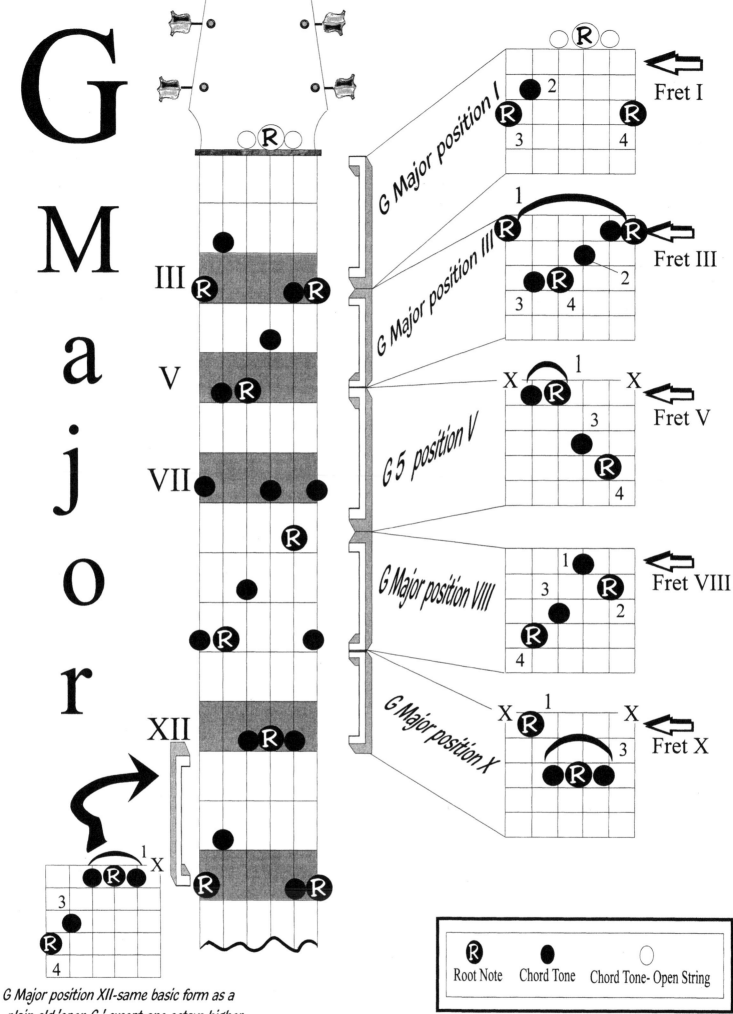

G Major

G Major position I — Fret I

G Major position III — Fret III

G 5 position V — Fret V

G Major position VIII — Fret VIII

G Major position X — Fret X

G Major position XII-same basic form as a
plain old 'open G' except one octave higher.

R	R	R
Root Note	Chord Tone	Chord Tone- Open String

The 5 basic shapes of C Major.

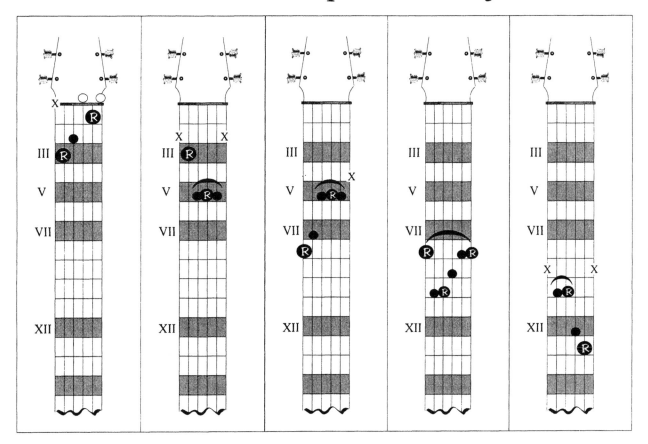

The 5 basic shapes of G Major.

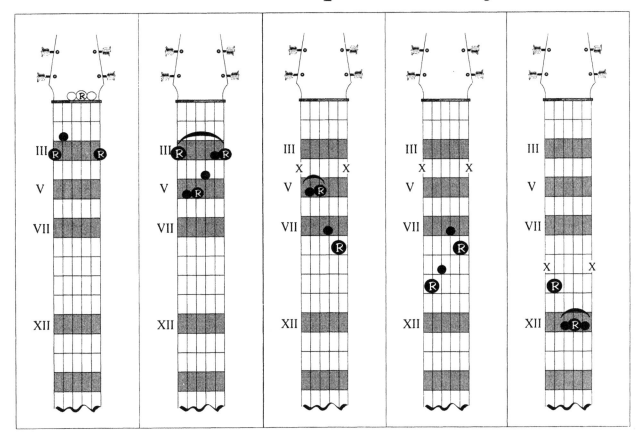

The 5 basic shapes of C Major.

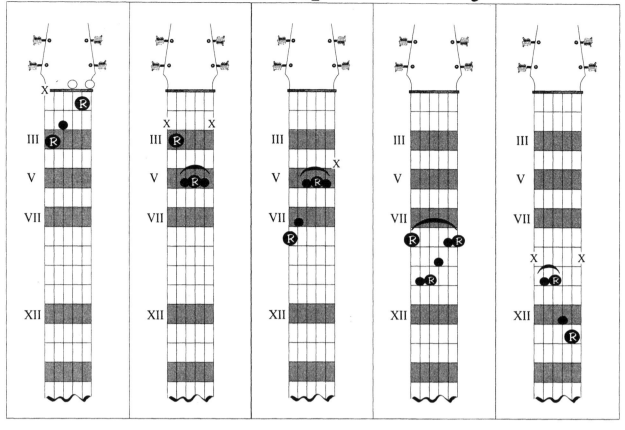

Open position   position III   position V   position VIII   position X

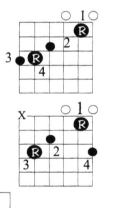

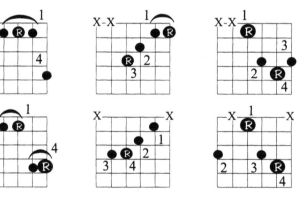

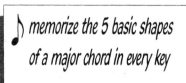

The concept of the 5 basic shapes is the industry standard among professional guitarists and teachers. In the columns below each one of the 5 basic *grips,* there are optional chord shapes diagrammed. These options are different voicings of the Major chord in the same position which are included here for the sake of completeness and for comparison of this book to other methods.

There really is not one "right way" to do this, just several excellent theories which examine and interpret the same fundamental facts we've outlined here.

The 5 main chord grips *I've* used as my base line system of reasoning are excellent for purposes of practicing, playing and learning to visualize each musical key up and down the entire neck.

♪ memorize the 5 basic shapes of a major chord in every key

♪ learn to convert these 5 shapes to minor & dominant
-pp.95 & 98.

O
P
T
I
O
N
S

First chord, up one octave

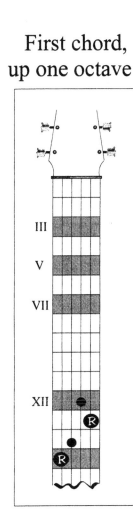

position XII

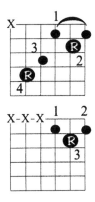

The sixth chord in the series has the same shape as the first one -except one octave higher in pitch. At this point, the pattern of 5 basic chords repeats .

The 5 basic chord shapes should be learned and practiced in all 12 keys. A thorough knowledge of the 5 chord grips is the foundation of advanced and professional guitar playing in all styles.

The ability to visualize a chord along the entire length of the guitar neck is absolutely necessary for playing hot lead guitar and rhythm grooves like those on recordings.

Practice playing the chords in successive order. Give each chord two beats as you ascend and descend through the pattern of the 5 grips.

As you practice the 5 shapes

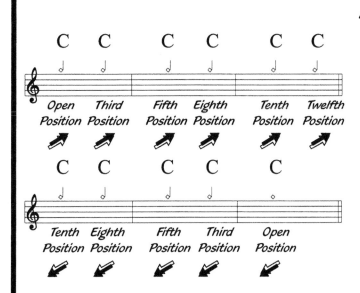

C	C	C	C	C	C
Open Position	Third Position	Fifth Position	Eighth Position	Tenth Position	Twelfth Position

C	C	C	C	C
Tenth Position	Eighth Position	Fifth Position	Third Position	Open Position

♪ KEEP THE BEAT

♪ Increase tempos daily

♪ locate root notes mentally

♪ play in all 12 keys

All top notch and professional guitarists play and know these 5 chords in all 12 keys. This is the key to organizing and understanding the true nature of the guitar. Playing up and down the neck in an effortless fashion is ultimately related to the 5 basic shapes. A mastery of this material is the first step towards becoming an excellent guitarist.

In this book, the 5 basic shapes of a Major chord are diagrammed in the keys of A, B, C, D, E, F & G.

The 5 basic shapes of A Major.

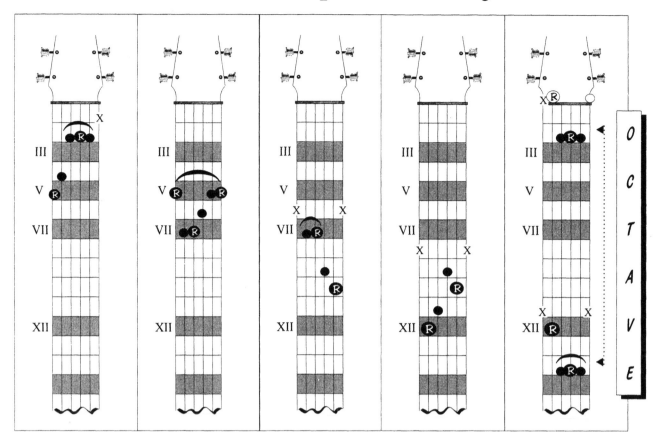

The 5 basic shapes of B Major.

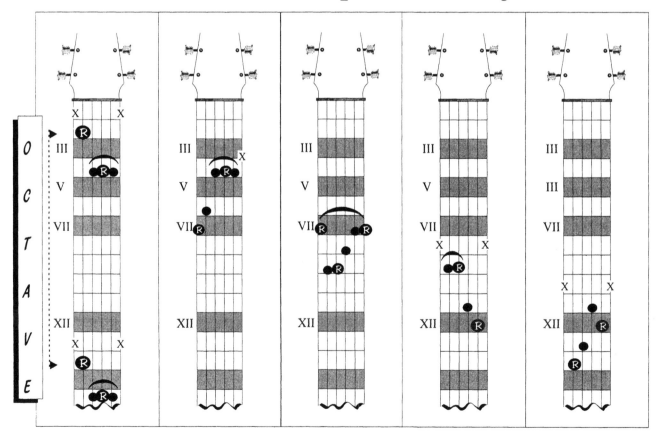

The 5 basic shapes of D Major.

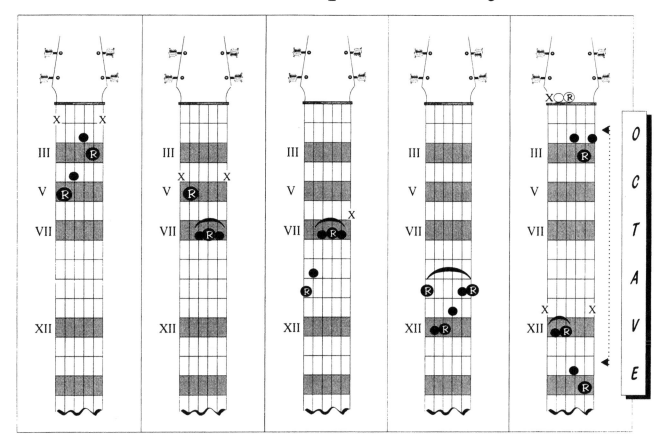

The 5 basic shapes of E Major.

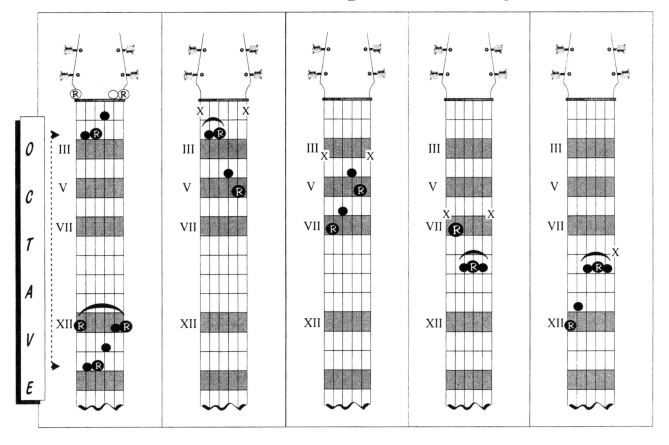

The 5 basic shapes of F Major.

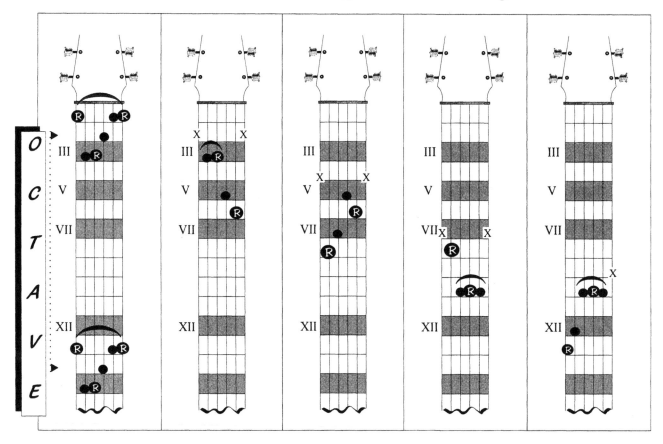

OCTAVE

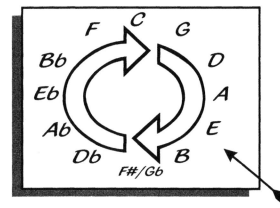

The critical thing about the 5 chords shapes is this:

THE SEQUENCE Of THE CHORDS NEVER CHANGES.

It's always the same 5 chords in the same order for every
key - in this regard, all 12 keys are the same.
- the only change is in location on the neck.

Using the circle of fifths as a
study tool, practice the 5 chord shapes
in tempo.

Exercises:

1.) Play all 5 chords in all 12
keys in tempo.

2.) Play one type of chord
fingering in 12 different
keys.

3.) Doing your best to **stay in
one position,** play Major chords
with 12 different root notes.

4.) Repeat *exercise 3* in 4
other spots on the neck.

Converting the 5 basic shapes to minor

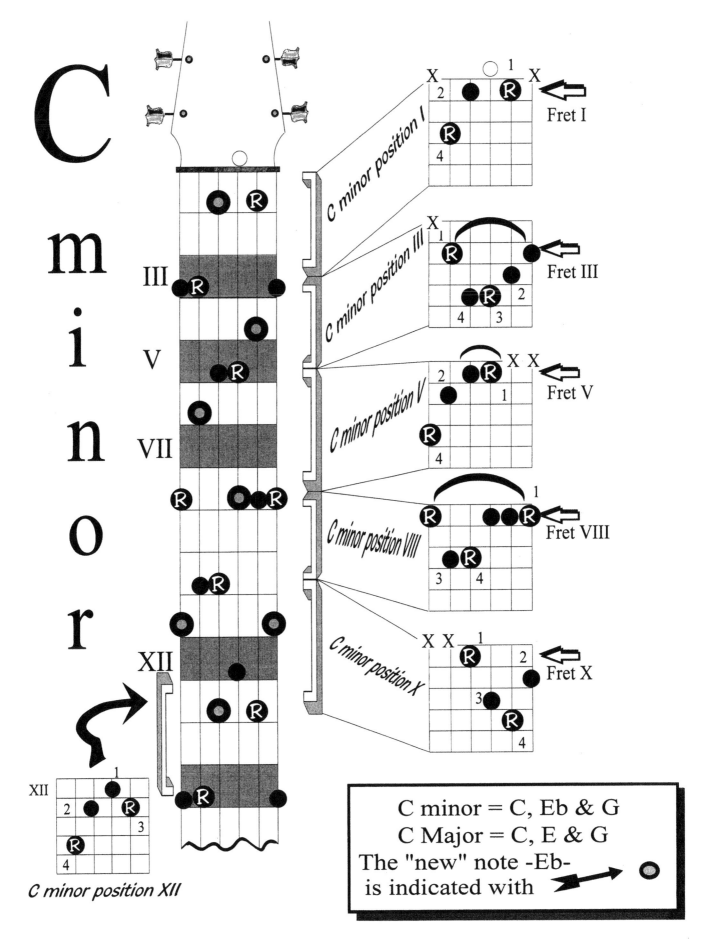

C minor position I — Fret I

C minor position III — Fret III

C minor position V — Fret V

C minor position VIII — Fret VIII

C minor position X — Fret X

C minor position XII

C minor = C, Eb & G
C Major = C, E & G
The "new" note -Eb-
is indicated with

The 5 basic shapes of A minor.

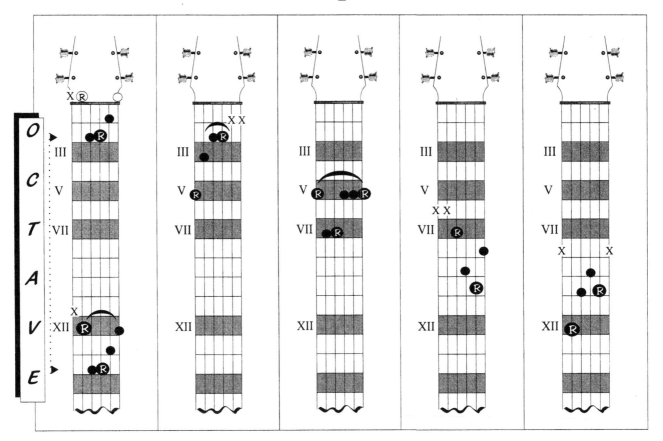

The 5 basic shapes of C minor.

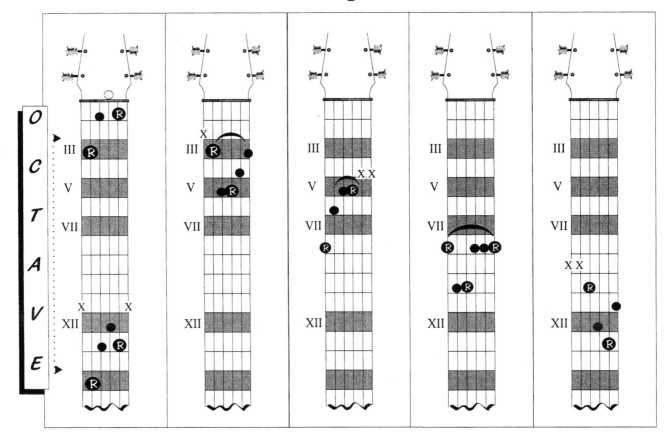

The 5 basic shapes of E minor.

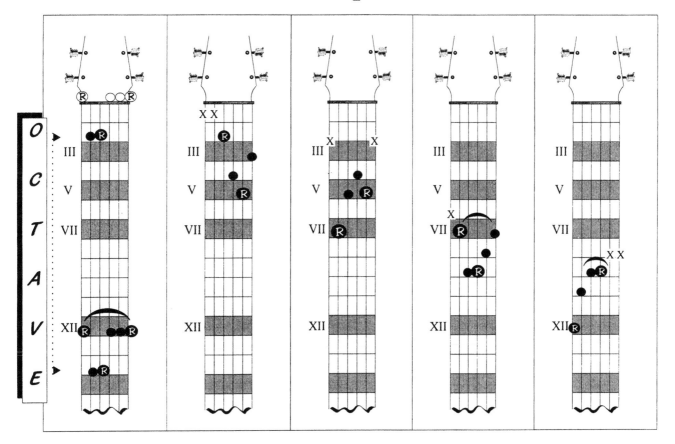

The 5 basic shapes of G minor.

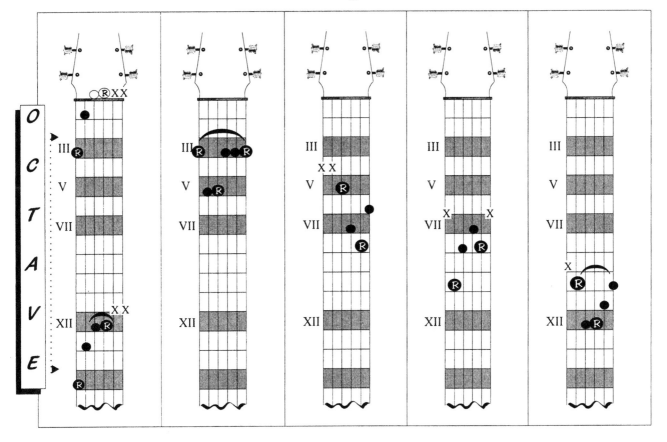

Converting the 5 basic shapes to dominant

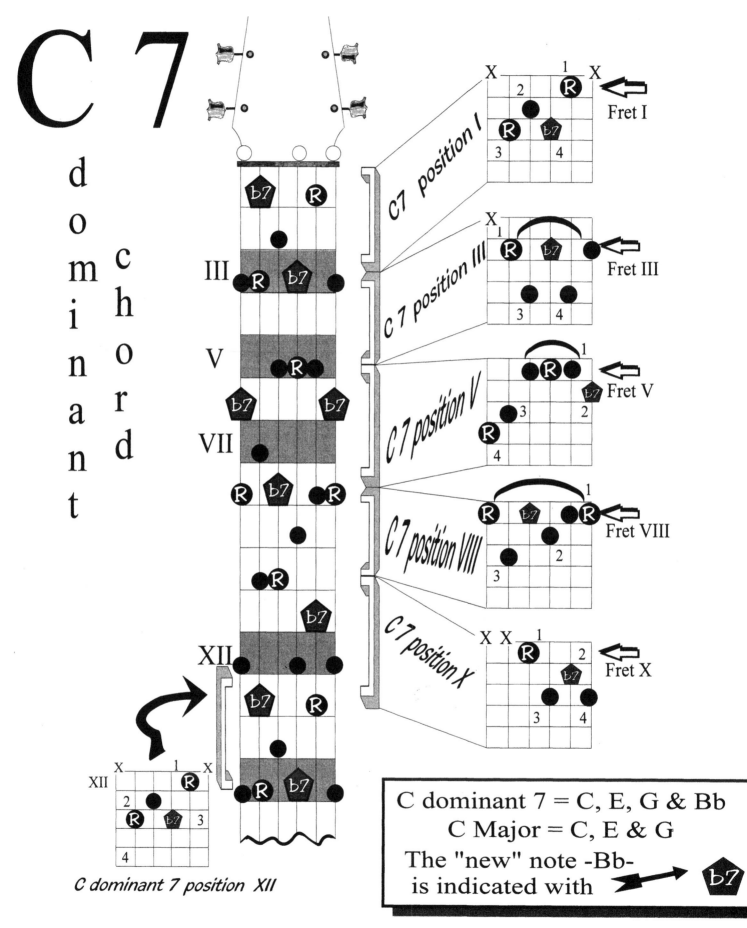

C 7
dominant chord

C7 position I

Fret I

c 7 position III

Fret III

C 7 position V

Fret V

C 7 position VIII

Fret VIII

C 7 position X

Fret X

C dominant 7 position XII

C dominant 7 = C, E, G & Bb
C Major = C, E & G
The "new" note -Bb-
is indicated with   b7

The 5 basic shapes of A7.

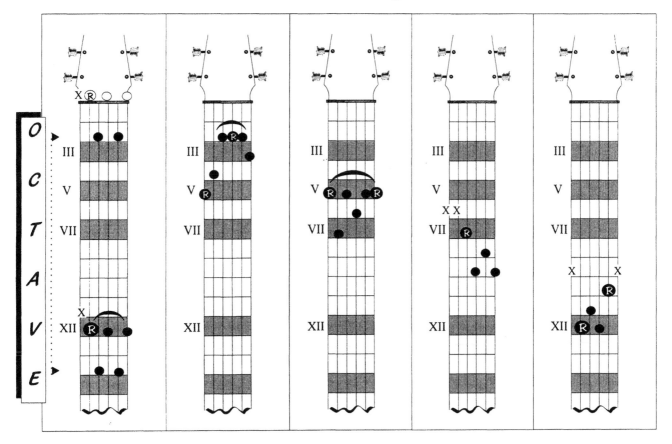

The 5 basic shapes of C7.

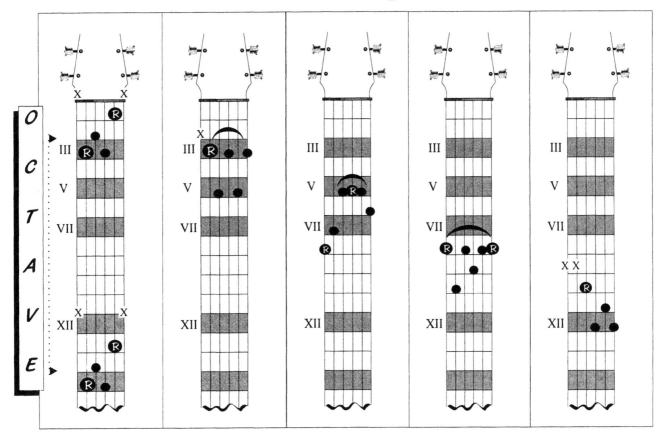

The 5 basic shapes of E 7.

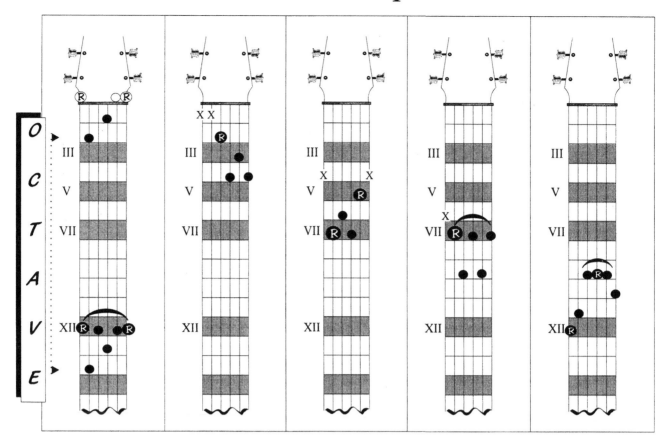

The 5 basic shapes of G 7

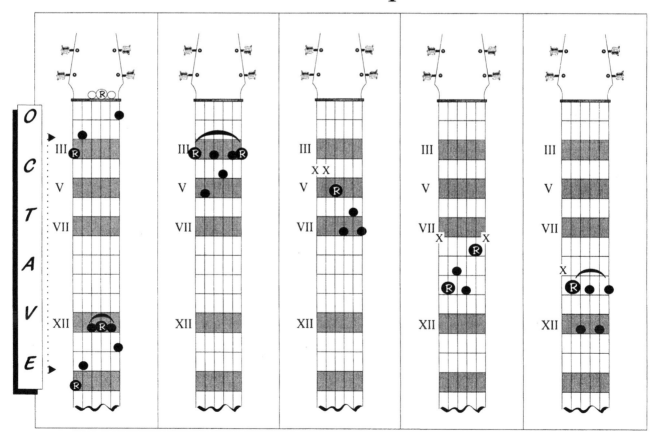

The 5 Chord shapes: Summary

If there were one concept that all accomplished guitarists were in agreement* on, it would be that of *5 position playing* as I've begun to outline here. Knowing the 5 basic chord shapes of a Major, minor & dominant chord in each of the 12 keys of music should be your top priority if you are at all serious about the guitar. Develop your own system of practicing using the box below as a guide:

Major	*minor*	*Dominant*

A A#/Bb B C C#/Db D D#/Eb E F F#/Gb G G#/Ab A

Exercises.

Play 5 positions of **A major** in tempo.....*take notice of all root notes.*

Play 5 positions of **A minor** in tempo......*take notice of all root notes.*

Play 5 positions of **A 7** in tempo......*take notice of all root notes.*

Play **C Major, C minor** & **C7** two beats each....

*Transpose
to all
12 keys.*

in the first position.
in the third position.
in the fifth position.
in the eighth position.
in the tenth position.
in the twelfth position.

A thought process: The 5 basic shapes in position I.

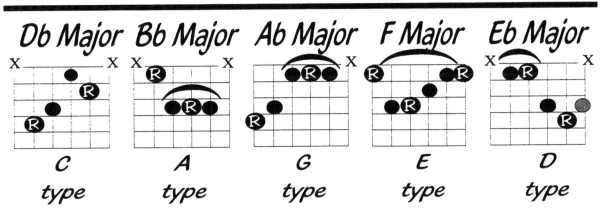

Db Major	Bb Major	Ab Major	F Major	Eb Major
C type	A type	G type	E type	D type

Above are the 5 basic shapes diagrammed in the 1st position. The actual "real life" name of the chord appears above the chord graph. The chord type or 'parent chord' is the type of basic open string chord this chord most closely resembles. This system was first written about in the 50's & 60's by ***William G. Leavitt, Jack Marshall*** and ***Howard Roberts***. Books by these great guitarists are essential to a complete library.

* A number of guitarists agreeing about anything is generally considered to be unusual.

Synonymous Chords

Sometimes the same chord form or shape can have more than one name and therefore more than one application. Below are the most useful synonymous chords in the key of C.

C- 6 ⟺ A-7⁽ᵇ⁵⁾

(1st)	C		A	(1st)
(b3rd)	Eb		C	(3rd)
(5th)	G		Eb	(b5th)
(6th)	A		G	(7th)

C 6 ⟺ A-7

(1st)	C		A	(1st)
(3rd)	E		C	(3rd)
(5th)	G		E	(5th)
(7th)	A		G	(7th)

CMa 7 ⟺ A-9

(1st)	C		A	(1st)
(3rd)	E		C	(b3rd)
(5th)	G		E	(5th)
(7th)	B		G	(7th)
			B	(9th)

Any chord known as C mi 6 can be used in any situation calling for A mi 7(b5).

Any chord known as A mi 7(b5) can be used in any situation calling for C mi 6.

Any chord known as C6 can be used in place of A mi 7.

Any chord known as A mi 7 can be used in any situation calling for C6.

Any chord known as C Ma 7 can be used in place of A mi 9.

Any chord known as A mi 9 can be used in place of C Ma 7.

The substitution of chords can be extremely effective and powerful provided you carefully listen to your playing. The golden rule of substituting chords is:

"When something sounds right, it is right"

Professional musicians listen very carefully to everything they do as a form of job security. Playing without ever listening to yourself guarantees that no else will ever listen to you either. If you **really like the sound** of something, your audience will like it to.

Table of Chord Substitutions

C6 = Ami 7	C ma7 =A mi 9*	C mi 6 = A mi 7 (b5)
Db6 = Bb mi 7	Db ma7 =Bb mi 9	Db mi 6 = Bb mi 7 (b5)
D6 = B mi 7	D ma7 =B mi 9	D mi 6 = B mi 7 (b5)
Eb6 = C mi 7	Eb ma7 =C mi 9	Eb mi 6 = C mi 7 (b5)
E6 = C# mi 7	E ma7 =C# mi 9	E mi 6 = C# mi 7 (b5)
F6 = D mi 7	F ma7 =D mi 9	F mi 6 = D mi 7 (b5)
Gb6 = Eb mi 7	Gb ma7 =Eb mi 9	Gb mi 6 = Eb mi 7 (b5)
G6 = E mi 7	Gma7 =E mi 9	G mi 6 = E mi 7 (b5)
Ab6 = F mi 7	Abma7 =F mi 9	Ab mi 6 = F mi 7 (b5)
A6 = F# mi 7	Ama7 =F# mi 9	A mi 6 = F# mi 7 (b5)
Bb6 = G mi 7	Bbma7 =G mi 9	Bb mi 6 = G mi 7 (b5)
B6 = G# mi 7	Bma7 =G# mi 9	B mi 6 = G# mi 7 (b5)

C Major 13

C E G B(7) D(9) A(13)

A minor 11

A C E G(7) B(9) D(11)

The extended harmonies of a **C Major** and an **A minor** contain essentially the same notes. This is the logic behind viewing **C Ma 7 & A mi 9** as substitutes.

Sus 2 vs. add 9 chords

C sus 2 =   **C** *(1)* **D** *(2)* **G** *(5)*

C add 9 =   **C** *(1)* **E** *(3)* **G** *(5)* **D** *(9)*

For playing purposes:
Any chord known as **C sus 2** can be used in any situation calling for **C add 9.**

C add 9 usually does the job of **C sus 2**, *unless your ear tells you otherwise.*

C add 9 — root 6

F sus 2 — root 5

A sus 2 — root 4

(see pages 54 & 55 for additional voicings)

Diminished 7 vs. Dominant 7 (b9) chords

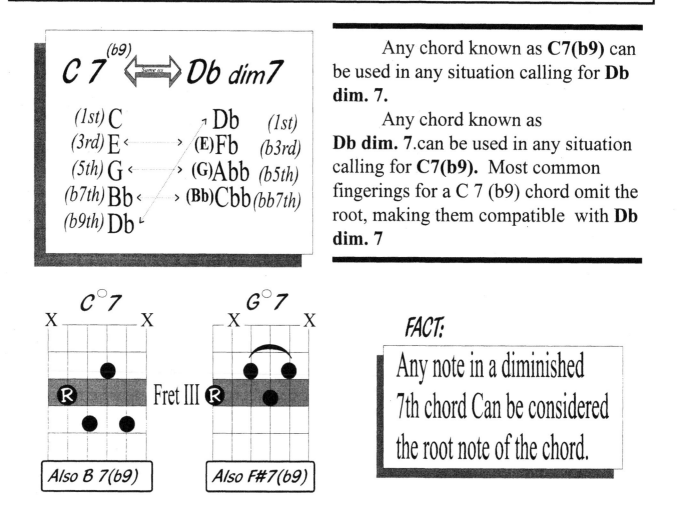

Any chord known as **C7(b9)** can be used in any situation calling for **Db dim. 7.**

Any chord known as **Db dim. 7.** can be used in any situation calling for **C7(b9).** Most common fingerings for a C 7 (b9) chord omit the root, making them compatible with **Db dim. 7**

FACT:

Any note in a diminished 7th chord Can be considered the root note of the chord.

SYNOMOUS CHORDS:

C **dim.7** = Eb dim.7 = Gb dim.7 = A dim.7

G **dim.7** = Bb dim.7 = Db dim.7 = E dim.7

C **7 (b9)** = Eb 7 (b9) = Gb 7 (b9) = A 7 (b9)

G **7 (b9)** = Bb 7 (b9) = Db 7 (b9) = E 7 (b9)

FACT:

In these dom. 7 (b9) chords, any note one fret below a chord tone can be considered the root note of the chord.